The Confirmation of the Gospel

J. Waskom Pickett

FOREWORD BY DR. JON KULAGA
INTRODUCTION BY DR. ARTHUR McPHEE

THE CONFIRMATION OF THE GOSPEL:
THE AUTHENTICATING ROLE OF GOOD WORKS

by
J. Waskom Pickett

Copyright ©2016 Asbury University
ISBN: 978-0-9963358-1-2
Printed in the United States of America
by Edwards Brothers Malloy
Ann Arbor, Mich.

INSTITUTIONAL MISSION

The mission of Asbury University, as a Christian liberal arts university in the Wesleyan-Holiness tradition, is to equip men and women, through a commitment to academic excellence and spiritual vitality, for a lifetime of learning, leadership and service to the professions, society, the family and the Church, thereby preparing them to engage their cultures and advance the cause of Christ around the world.

COVER: *Three of the works of mercy (giving drink to the thirsty, visiting the prisoner, clothing the naked) as depicted in a large Romanesque icon of the Last Judgment. It was painted in the second half of the 12th century for the oratory of St. Gregory Nazianzen near Santa Maria in Campo Marzio. It is now part of the collection of the Vatican Museums.*

TABLE OF CONTENTS

Foreword 4
by Dr. Jon Kulaga

"J. Waskom Picket: A Brief Biography" 6
by Dr. Arthur McPhee

Preface.. 14

Chapter 1 17
The Need for Confirmation

Chapter 2 31
Confirmation Through the Healing Ministry

Chapter 3 45
Confirmation Through Changed Lives

Chapter 4 61
Confirmation Through the Resurrection

Chapter 5 73
Confirmation by the Holy Spirit

Chapter 6 85
Confirmation Through the Church

Chapter 7 99
The Continuing Need for Confirmation

Acknowledgements 115

FOREWORD

In the spring of 2015, Asbury University established *The Foundry*, an online repository of faculty and student research, as well as historical materials from the University Library Archives and Special Collections. Over the summer of 2015, Morgan Tracy, Director of Library Services, and Suzanne Gehring, Director of the University Archives, started analyzing the University's collections of historical materials to determine: 1) what would be of value to researchers if digitized and available online and 2) what had not already been digitized by someone else. The Pickett Collection seemed to be a great place to start. The J. Waskom Pickett Collection consists of over 9 linear feet of papers including family historical material; correspondence; materials having to do with the Methodist Church in India and the United States; manuscripts of books, speeches, sermons and articles; and scrapbooks, photos, slides, and artifacts. Bishop and Mrs. Pickett's children gave the collection to the University on August 2, 1982.

During this analysis, the manuscript for "The Confirmation of the Gospel," was discovered, along with correspondence from Abingdon Press, which had essentially declined it for publication due to its brevity. After consulting with Dr. Arthur McPhee's seminal biography "The Road to Delhi: J. Waskom Pickett Remembered", it was confirmed that the text had never been published, and that it reflected some of Pickett's best thought on integrating social and spiritual needs.

The Confirmation of the Gospel

In the making of this book, the hope is to introduce a new audience to one of Asbury University's "great alums", and also one of Methodism's greatest missionary bishops. The short biography provided by Dr. McPhee that precedes the actual text by Pickett will give the reader a glimpse into the breadth, depth, and scope of Rev. Pickett's international influence and ministry. It is also hoped that the message of the work itself will inspire readers to understand and live out the "indivisible link" between personal holiness and social holiness. Finally, it is also hoped that through this and other works researchers of church growth, missiology, etc. will be encouraged to utilize not only the entire Pickett Collection, but all the historical materials of the University's Archives and Special Collections.

Jon S. Kulaga, Ph.D.
Provost
Gardner Professor for the Promotion of Holiness
Asbury University

February 14, 2016

J. WASKOM PICKETT: A BRIEF BIOGRAPHY

When, in 1906, Jarrell Waskom Pickett was 16 and working on his Master's Degree at Asbury College, Miss Elizabeth Sheffield Allen, a graduate of the University of Tennessee and the Curry School in Boston, came to head up what the college called its "Expression Department." Her classroom tutelage, however, was only one of a mix of opportunities available to young Waskom for shaping and sharpening his speaking skills. There was also the student-run Boy's Conference, which met after classes each day for critiquing 15-minute practice addresses. Then there were the oratorical contests sponsored by Asbury's chapter of the International Prohibition Society. And debate training came as a feature of Asbury's two literary societies. Waskom was a member of the Columbian Society. One of Waskom's college-days speeches found its way into the Pentecostal Herald, the best-known Holiness paper of the day. Here is a sample:

"In whatsoever calling he is found, let every man therein abide with Christ. Let him use the carpenter's bench, the merchant's desk, the artist's studio, the Governor's mansion, the senator's chair, the palace or the throne as the pulpit from which to preach Jesus. Preach him by tongue and pen, by devoted life, by godly example, by precept and practice, by service and sacrifice."

Given his rhetorical knowhow and practice, Waskom no doubt felt well-prepared for winning lost souls to Christ by the power of his words. And, his initial success as a missionary in India seemed to confirm it. At the Lal Bagh English Church in Lucknow, to which he was assigned in 1910, the young Reverend Pickett's preaching was warmly received by the members – mostly missionary colleagues, other expatriates, and Anglo-Indians. And although he found open-air preaching more difficult, his solution was simply "preparation":

"There is a feeling that one can preach in the bazaars and melas and that no sort of preparation is necessary. Pastors who would not think of appearing before their congregations without hours of preparation, if they engage in open-air preaching at all . . . begin to speak without having more than the haziest idea of what they will say."

During his second term in India, however, during which he was assigned to rural Bihar, Pickett grew in his conviction that the gospel must be proclaimed by devoted life, godly example, service, and sacrifice as well as words. In Bihar, Pickett, now married with children, saw close-up the unhappy effects of destitution and disease, famine and floods, and caste and class distinctions. He knew instinctively that the gospel to live up to its meaning – good news – had to be good news for today, not just for the afterlife. That meant it had to be lived as well as taught.

Still, words were required, both for pointing to Jesus and for explaining that Christian love and compassion spring from the love and compassion of Jesus Christ. Without that explanation, one could by deeds of love only succeed in pointing to one's self. Thus, loving words were necessary for interpreting the deeds, just as loving deeds were necessary for confirming the words. To

Pickett, they were of one cloth.

These convictions became more widely apparent in Pickett's third missionary term, when he served as editor of Methodism's widely read "Indian Witness." Week after week his editorials and article selections reflected his two-fold commitment to proclamation in word and deed. One week he would write about a new way of open-air preaching using informal, friendly sermonettes of three to six minutes interspersed with *bhajans* or *gazals* (Indian songs). The next week he would write about the neglect of children, abuse of servants, or callous views of poverty. To someone's remark that "God must love poor folks since he made so many of them," he rejoined, "God is blamed for a great many things for which He is not responsible." He allowed that "there are a lot of poor people in the world and God made them all," but he reminded his readers, "[God] did not make them all poor" and chastised those who amassed riches on the backs of the destitute. He warned that even those "with high standards of personal morality . . . are crushing others under an appalling load of poverty." How? "By sinful practices in industries which they control."

In 1928, Pickett had a visit from John R. Mott, which a few months later, led to Pickett's involvement in something entirely new: conducting a study of conversion movements to Christianity, in which village caste groups – mostly outcastes – embraced the gospel as a unit. Since more than 80 percent of all those who had come into Indian Protestant and Catholic churches were untouchables, and since controversy concerning the judiciousness of promoting group conversion movements had persisted for years, a serious study of them was of no small importance.

Under the auspices of the National Christian Council of India, and with the sponsorship and technical assistance of the Institute of Social and Religious Research in New York, Pickett led survey teams that interviewed more than four thousand so-called "mass movement" Christians. The survey would be the first of three and lead to numerous reports and three books, including "Christian Movements in Mid India" (1938) and "Christ's Way to India's Heart" (1938). The volume resulting from the initial survey – more than three hundred pages of data, findings, conclusions, and recommendations concerning the conversion movements – appeared in 1933. It was greeted with a chorus of praise. One missionary colleague, Dr. Donald A. McGavran, read it and wrote, "There has come a book sent by God, and its name is 'Christian Mass Movements in India'."

To exaggerate the impact of Pickett's research and conclusions on the Indian church scene would not be easy. It caused many mission boards and Indian churches to rethink and alter their priorities and methods. McGavran, who said of Pickett, "I lit my candle at his fire," became famous as the father of the Church Growth Movement by extending Pickett's findings and recommendations to the global scene.

A review of social surveys up to that time shows Pickett's study to be the most ambitious one of its kind ever attempted outside the West. The interviews he and his colleagues conducted resulted in the largest database ever amassed on untouchable believers. More important, though, was the survey's legitimization of employing the social sciences for research on evangelization. Up to that time, theology alone mattered. Now, however, the social sciences were seen to have a role in evangelistic thinking, strategy, and assessment – and not an incidental one. Research and getting the facts down were now seen as essential tools for laying bare false assumptions and putting the missionary enterprise on a more substantial foundation.

In August 1947, the British granted independence to India while dividing it into two nations: the secular state of India dominated by Hindus, and Muslim Pakistan. Interreligious violence broke out on both sides of the new borders, forcing millions to evacuate their lifelong homes and emigrate. Violence and retribution broke out on the travel routes as well. To save Muslim lives in Delhi, Pickett, now the senior Methodist bishop in India and former president of India's National Christian Council, oversaw the establishment and administration of a number of refugee camps. As a result, tens of thousands of lives were saved. Donald Ebright, onetime Director of Famine Relief for the National Christian Council of India, wrote that during the communal riots following Independence and Partition, "Bishop J. W. Pickett . . . did more than any one non-government person to organize voluntary relief in Delhi."

Following independence, no expatriate in India surpassed Pickett in political influence. Although their relationship could occasionally be contentious, Pickett and Gandhi knew each other well. Located in Delhi, Bishop Pickett had unusual access to Prime Minister Nehru, knew all the members of his cabinet, and was a close friend of B. R. Ambedkar, Nehru's Law Minister and Rajkumari Amrit Kaur, his Health Minister. There is good evidence that H. C. Mookerjee, Vice President of India's Constituent Assembly and chair of the session that adopted the religious liberties clause of India's constitution, sought Pickett's advice on some of the language for that section. Unlike any other constitution, India's specifically gives the right to "propagate" one's faith, although, in practice, India's states have often disregarded it.

In the 1950s, Pickett met with two U.S. presidents on behalf of India: (1) with Truman in 1950 to plead for a policy change that would allow the sale of American surplus wheat to prevent widespread famine; and (2) with Eisenhower in 1954 to urge a shift from the disastrous policies of Secretary of State John Foster Dulles favoring Pakistan. During those same years, he also organized and became the first president of the United Mission to Nepal, one of the most inventive models of ecumenical mission ever employed.

Among Pickett's greatest contributions in India was his work in establishing hospitals, tuberculosis sanitariums, clinics and medical training programs. According to the pioneering field surgeon, Dr. Charles Perrill, in the last half of the twentieth century, J. Waskom Pickett advanced medical care in India more than any other individual. Having experienced God's healing himself after contracting tuberculosis in 1914, Pickett worked tirelessly to better the health prospects of others. He regarded ministries of healing as an essential means of confirming the Good News and serving Christ.

In early May, 1948, Waskom spoke at the Convention for the Deepening of the Spiritual Life at the most beautiful of the southern hill stations, Kodaikanal. More than a mile high, it was the setting for an international boarding school and was surrounded by woodlands with wonderful walking trails and a lake. It was on a lake and was a favored vacation spot for missionaries. Pickett called his addresses, "The Confirmation of the Gospel." It was at least the second time he had chosen the theme, and the following year he would develop a small book on it, which, until now, never was published. As the reader of this volume will discover, it contains important insights on the indivisible link in gospel proclamation between compassionate words and deeds.

After forty-six years, Pickett retired from missionary service in 1956. He told his friends, "We are leaving home and going to America." He and his wife, Ruth Robinson Pickett moved to New England, where, for several years, he was the professor of missions at Boston University's School of Theology. When he was not teaching, he traveled the world representing the Methodist mission board. J. Waskom Pickett died at Columbus, Ohio in 1981 at age ninety-one.

Arthur McPhee, Ph.D.
Sundo Kim Professor of Evangelism and Practical Theology
Asbury Theological Seminary

The Confirmation of the Gospel

PREFACE

This book began to take shape when I prepared a series of addresses for a Convention for the Deepening of the Spiritual Life held at Kodaikanal, South India, in May, 1949. It advanced to approximately its present form as the Willson Lectures delivered at McMurry College, Abilene, Texas, in March, 1950. But the thinking that finds expression here has an earlier origin. I began my missionary work in India in 1910 with an exaggerated idea of the effectiveness of preaching as an evangelizing force, and went through a period of disillusionment. The plainer I made my preaching of the Gospel the more decisively my Hindu and Muslim hearers rejected it. Reluctantly and very slowly I came to a realization of the fact that the Gospel, that seemed to me so beautiful and appealing, was to most of my hearers entirely incredible. I knew then that I must revise my program or remain ineffective. In desperation I turned to the records of the ministry of Jesus as written by Matthew, Mark, Luke and John and studied them afresh in the hope of finding how our Lord sought to win converts. My first discovery amazed me. It was that Jesus did not rely to any large extent upon preaching, and that His preaching was not especially effective. He spent more time in teaching a few than in preaching to crowds. And His healing ministry, rather than His preaching, drew the crowds. In fact, His preaching sometimes repelled groups that had been drawn to Him by reports of His service to the afflicted.

Jewish hearers of the Gospel from the lips of the Master found it as difficult as do Hindus and Muslims in the India of our times to believe the Gospel. It seems that few would have listened to His sermons but for the attraction exercised upon them by His good works. I came to the conviction that a good minister of Jesus Christ in India, where human need approximates closely to that which Jesus confronted in Palestine, finds no authority, in the example or mandate of this Lord, for preaching isolated from good works. To ignore physical needs and preach is to deny the Gospel, while success depends upon confirming it.

The Confirmation of the Gospel

CHAPTER I

The Need for Confirmation

The Confirmation of the Gospel

The Gospel must be confirmed. It is not enough to proclaim it. Jesus, the completely authoritative exponent of the Gospel and the most persuasive of preachers, never regarded preaching as sufficient. Wherever He went He confirmed His mighty Word with wondrous works.

St. Mark tells us that in His preaching Jesus called upon the people to repent and believe the Gospel. They were astonished because He taught them as one that had authority and not as the scribes. But unlike some of His modern disciples, He did not consider that His duty was done when He had preached, so that the responsibility was then upon His hearers to accept or reject His message. He thought that those who heard Him were entitled to proof that what He said was true, so He confirmed the Gospel. He healed the sick, cleansed the lepers, cast out evil spirits, gave sight to the blind, preached to the poor and thus by word and deed made what He preached credible.

Why did Jesus provide confirmation of His preaching? Why did He not demand its acceptance by faith without reasoning? That is exactly what many religious teachers have done, but it can never be done consistently with the Gospel because of the nature of the Gospel. Because God is as Jesus represented Him to be, His Message must be presented with due respect for the hearer's personality. He who said, "Love God with all your mind" would not ask for the acceptance of His message and mission without cause or reason.

Furthermore, Jesus found it necessary to confirm the Gospel, because without confirmation few would believe it. The simple fact is that to most of His hearers what He told them was incredible. Even those who heard Him gladly rarely believed that what He said was true. We who have heard the Gospel from early childhood seldom realize how strange it seemed to those who first heard it, or how incredible it sounds today to people first schooled in the tenets of another faith.

The Scribes, most of the Pharisees and all of the Sadducees seem to have recognized His preaching as a menace to their privileged positions. They did not want to believe that God was no respecter of persons or that God is love in His dealings with all men. Their cherished leadership was acknowledged because of the belief, which they sedulously propagated, that they were God's deserving favorites. It is not surprising then that they rejected the Gospel. On the other hand, the common people, poor, neglected and exploited, recognized Him as their defender, benefactor and friend. Yet even they found it very difficult to believe His Gospel. They came to hear Him preach. In throngs they brought their sick and handicapped loved ones and neighbors to Him for healing, but there was no rush to accept or act upon His Gospel. Even the disciples who left their homes and families to go with this strange and wonderful man found His preaching not entirely convincing. He often had to rebuke them for their unbelief. Ordinarily they did not confess their unbelief and they never argued with the Master. Possibly they did not even formulate in their own minds a statement of their dissent. But when testing situations developed, their unbelief was revealed.

At the heart of the Gospel is what Jesus taught about the character of God, that He is holy and has no part in man's sins, and that He is loving and does not turn against men because of their sins. It has never been easy for men to bring the ideas of God's holiness and His love into harmonious relation one with another. Either they have thought that a holy God was angry with men for their sins, or that a loving God was indifferent to sins committed by His favorites and that He was Himself capable of doing all manner of evil for the sake of those whom He loved. Some have imagined God to be unstable, even whimsical, in His attitudes toward men and have supposed holiness and love to be incompatible and mutually exclusive.

Almost every sin known to man has been attributed by man to God as having been done to further His purposes for those whom He has loved. Among the people with whom Jesus lived and to whom He preached in Galilee and Judaea probably a majority believed that God often made children blind because He was angry with one of their parents, grandparents or even more distant ancestors. Prevailing thought interpreted all suffering as due to the wrath of God. Even the disciples, long after their training began, asked Jesus, "Master, who did sin, this man or his parents, that he was born blind?" And Jesus answered, "Neither hath this man sinned nor his parents, but that the works of God might be manifest in him." Jesus was certainly not suggesting that this man and his parents had been free from sin, but that the blindness had not been sent upon him, as the disciples and the people generally believed, because God was angry over his sins or the sins of his parents. Neither was Jesus suggesting that the man had been made blind in order that the power of God might be revealed in his healing. What He was saying in effect was, "It is not the will of God that he should be blind. I will show you what the will of God for him is. The works of God will be made manifest in him. I must work the works of Him that sent me." And thus saying, He healed the man of his blindness.

The essence of the Good News that Jesus preached was this: "God is not against any man for his sins. He is for every man against his sins." This teaching made the Scribes and Pharisees exceedingly angry. Probably many of them were alarmed at what they thought would be the bad effects of this preaching. Their alarm was the greater because they saw that Jesus was acting in accord with this idea – He was going to the homes of sinners, eating with them and seemingly enjoying their company. He spoke tenderly to those whom they were accustomed to denounce and reserved His severest language for them. They thought of themselves as people who pleased God and believed that a true minister of God would, of necessity, recognize them as more deserving than those whom they branded as sinners, and consequently would prefer to associate with and honor them. Given their understanding of the character of God, they were right. But Jesus knew better. He preached that God was different, and by His actions in dealing with people, He confirmed His preaching.

Even the disciples, after months of intimate association with Jesus, found it difficult to accept the Gospel of a love that will never let go. After they had heard Him preach that Gospel and had seen Him confirm it in many miracles and in gentle, loving dealing with many sinners, their unbelief was still so evident that one day Jesus tried another method of helping them to understand the character of God. In rapid succession He told them three parables.

First came the parable of the good shepherd and the lost sheep. The shepherd, having a hundred sheep, loses one. He doesn't say, "Never mind. Ninety-nine are safe. I've done very well and we'll get along all right with these." Neither does he say, "That wicked sheep! I tried as hard to teach him as any of the others. He knew he should stay with the flock, but he strayed off. Now he is lost. It's all his fault." No, because he was a good shepherd, he didn't sit at ease and blame the lost sheep, but went out into the wilderness and hunted until he found the sheep and then brought him in rejoicing. "That" said Jesus, in effect, "is what God is like. God and His angels rejoice when a sinner is saved."

Then followed the parable of the faithful wife and the lost coin. I am glad that Jesus called attention to a good woman to help His disciples understand the true character of God. Lesser minds have not had the courage or the clarity of understanding necessary to do that. A woman having ten coins to meet the household expenses for the week loses one. She doesn't sit down in comfort and blame the coin. Neither does she say, "Never mind. I still have nine coins and will manage well enough. We'll eat a little less and John will wait until next week for his new shoes." No! Because she is a faithful wife and a good mother she hunts for that coin determined to do her full duty to her household. And when she finds it she calls her neighbors to rejoice with her. "That" said Jesus, in effect, "is what God is like. Men have been wrong in supposing that He was so different."

Lest even then the truth not be fully grasped, Jesus continued with the parable of the loving father and the ungrateful foolish son. This is commonly called "The Parable of the Prodigal Son," but that title obscures the meaning of the parable. It centers attention on the son, whereas the primary subject is the father. Its purpose is to show again what God is like.

A certain father had two sons. The younger became very difficult and treated the father badly. He demanded that the family estate be divided. He would take his share and live apart. He would show his stupid father how farming should be done and he'd get forever free from the old man's interference. The father did not have to yield to the demand, but he loved the lad and respected his personality so much that he would not rule over him against his wishes. The boy must learn. So he gave him his share and let him go. The selfish son left home very proud of his possessions and thinking little of the hurt he had given his father. He planned to buy land some distance away where it was cheaper, and when he was rich, he'd come back home to show off his wealth or he'd have his parents and older brother visit him. But his fond dreams didn't come true. He fell among evil companions and learned their ways. He drank and caroused while waiting for the opportunity to buy land. The opportunity was slow in coming, and he was having too good a time to leave his friends and go out to hunt for it. His money dwindled rapidly until one day he awoke to find it all gone and his friends angrily leaving him, and the inn-keeper demanding that he get more money or leave. And then famine smote the land. He could get no job. He was hungry. He sold his clothes. At last in rage, starving and dejected, he agreed to feed a rich man's pigs for a share of their food. He knew then how foolish he had been and how badly he had treated his father. Now the home, where he by his folly had made himself so unhappy, became in his thinking a wonderful place. "How many hired servants of my father's have bread enough and to spare and I perish with hunger! I will arise and go to my father and will say unto him, 'Father, I have sinned against Heaven and before thee, and am no more worthy to be called thy son. Make me as one of thy hired servants.'"

The son arose and went to his father. And the father was on the road looking for him, and ran to meet him and received him not as a servant but as the beloved son. He was not against the boy for his sins. He was for the boy, against all that his sins had done to him. He fed him the best he had, clothed him as he had never been clothed before, and gave him every good gift at his disposal. "That" said Jesus, in effect, "is what God is like. That is the Gospel I preach to you."

The difficulty experienced by the disciples at this point is shared by many thoughtful Hindus today. A national leader in India said to me a few years ago, "Your Christian doctrine that God loves all men and wishes to save them from sin is very attractive, but I don't believe it. God is too great to be concerned with individuals. And furthermore, the idea is dangerous. If people think their sins can be forgiven, they will abandon themselves to a life of sin." I pointed out that the idea that God is angry with men for their sins hasn't made many men refrain from sinning, nor has the belief that sin cannot be forgiven had any such effect. Actually, the strongest deterrent against wrong doing that men anywhere have experienced is the Christian Gospel of God's enduring love, leading Christ to His death on the cross that they might by faith in Him be saved. A Hindu Superintendent of Police in South India told me that the most criminal community in his district, Untouchable Outcastes, had, within twenty years, as a result of a Christian Mass Movement, become completely free from crime. "Moreover," he said, "they have changed from the dirtiest and most stupid people in the district into serious contenders with the Brahmans for the honor of being the cleanest and most intelligent of our citizens."

There are other records of the incredulity with which followers of Jesus heard the Gospel message from His lips. When He told them that they were dependent on Him for salvation and gave them the first intimation of the approaching sacrament of the broken body and shed blood some of His disciples said, "This is a hard saying; who can hear it?" And many of them so completely rejected what He had said that they "went back and walked no more with Him."

St. John tells us that after this His brethren urged Him, "Depart hence and go into Judaea that thy disciples may see the works that thou doest." "If thou doest these things, show thyself to the world." They recognized the value of His ministry of works as a confirmation of His preaching and teaching. Some who believed said, "Will Christ, when he cometh, do more miracles than these which this man hath done?"

Nicodemus, who liked Jesus, nevertheless frankly and vigorously rejected His doctrine of the new birth. To him it seemed incredible, if not absurd. "How can a man be born when he is old? Can he enter the second time into his mother's womb and be born?" That sounded conclusive. Jesus recognized as much and did not rebuke Nicodemus, but appreciating his difficulty, explained the doctrine.

Every missionary learns that many of those to whom he preaches have difficulty in believing much of his message. The sinlessness of Jesus, the forgiveness of sins, the uniqueness of Jesus as the Savior, and the need for the Church and its congregational worship have elicited most unbelief. A great Hindu leader, fearful lest his countrymen forsake Hinduism, argued that Jesus was a sinner like all other humans. When pressed to state wherein the record shows that Jesus committed sin he replied, "My most serious indictment of Jesus is that He showed no reverence for the cow." Thank God that Jesus showed no reverence for the cow! That same man later acknowledged that Jesus had influenced him as no one else had done, because His wonderful teaching and preaching was to such an extent proved by what He did and how He lived and died.

The Muslim often seems to be sorry for the Christian because the latter believes what to the former is so absurdly impossible. How often I have sat down with an educated Muslim, well-versed in the Koran and in Islamic traditions, and noticed him striving to be courteous and respectful while I have expounded what he regarded as incredible and foolish! Sometimes he has seemingly found it difficult to refrain from saying, "You poor foolish man! How can you believe these things?" The Muslim cannot be brought to Christ by preaching alone. For him the Gospel must be confirmed.

In Pakistan I questioned a young Muslim who had just been converted. "What made you want to be a Christian?" I asked. "The proof of the Gospel that I saw in the lives of the converted Untouchables," he replied. "I agreed with my uncle, who is the leading Muslim of my village, that the teaching seems unreasonable but when those worthless men and women, whom we all knew to be wicked and stupid, became our most trusted and honored neighbors I knew the Gospel was true. I wanted a religion that would save me, not just one that would sound reasonable." More recently in India an older Muslim who once was President of a Provincial branch of the Muslim League asked for baptism. He said, "I am forsaking Islam because it doesn't work and adopting the Christian faith because it does work. I saw both of these facts proved during the post-partition disturbances when Muslims killed and were killed in vast multitudes and Christians risked their lives to rescue both Muslims and their Sikh and Hindu attackers." This man has not yet made his public profession of Christian faith, but is one of a vast number who are restrained by community ties from action to which their minds and hearts incline them.

Many Hindus find it just as difficult to accept the Gospel as do the Muslims, but because of the great variety of Hindu beliefs there is no typical Hindu attitude as there is a Muslim attitude. Those central concepts of Hindu thought, awagaman (transmigration of the soul) and karma (accumulated merit or demerit determining the course of life) impel many Hindus to reject the great affirmations of the Gospel of Christ. If to you and me awagaman and karma seem absurd, I assure you that to many Hindu minds they appear to be the noblest triumphs of human reasoning and altogether credible. They so condition many Hindu minds as to make the entire teaching of Jesus about the persistent love of God for the unworthy and about salvation through faith in a Savior's death quite incomprehensible and unbelievable. The only way such Hindus are won to Christ is through the confirming of the Gospel, the offering of convincing evidence that it is true.

Jesus boldly presented His works as proof of His oneness with God and of the truth of what He preached and taught. When John the Baptist sent two of his disciples to ask, "Art thou He that should come or look we for another?" Jesus performed many wondrous works in their presence, then answering said, "Go your way and tell John what things ye have seen and heard, how that the blind see, the lame walk, the lepers are cleansed, the deaf hear, the dead are raised, to the poor the Gospel is preached." Not to John and his disciples alone, but to throngs He interpreted His works as a confirmation of His Word. "Believe me that I am in the Father and the Father in me, or else believe me for the very works' sake." When certain of the scribes complained on hearing Him say to a man sick of the palsy, "Thy sins be forgiven thee," He immediately announced that He would heal the man in order that they might know that He had the power to forgive sin. And at His command the sick man arose, took up his bed, and departed to his house.

Another feature of the Gospel which those who heard Jesus found hard to believe was the teaching that God is immanent and knowable. "The Kingdom of Heaven is at hand." Jesus repeatedly said, in effect, "God is not far off and unknowable and unconcerned about things that happen to the individual as you suppose. He is near, much closer than you have realized, is interested not in the nation only but in you and wants you to know, love and trust Him as your Creator and Father. To Him you are very precious." "The very hairs of your head are numbered." "Are not two sparrows sold for a farthing? And one of them shall not fall on the ground without your Father (caring).... Ye are of more value than many sparrows." "Behold the fowls of the air: for they sow not, neither do they reap, nor gather into barns; yet your Heavenly Father feedeth them. Are ye not much better than they?" "Consider the lilies of the field, how they grow; they toil not, neither do they spin: and yet I say unto you that even Solomon in all his glory was not arrayed like one of these. Wherefore if God so clothe the grass of the field which today is and tomorrow is cast into the oven, shall He not much more clothe you, O ye of little faith? .... For your Heavenly Father knoweth that ye have need of all these things. Seek ye first the Kingdom of God and all these things shall be added unto you."

Jesus preached this Gospel and patiently proved it to His disciples. He trusted God as Father and demonstrated day by day the truth of all He preached, showing how God cared not only for Him and His disciples, but for the sick and hungry and sinful people whom they were continually meeting.

No people are easily convinced of this Gospel. In India I have seen that people generally hear it with more interest than respect and more respect than belief. They sacrifice to God, as the Jews did, to win His favor. The priests in the temples ring bells before the idols to wake up Him whom they say they worship and gain His attention. "I wish God were like you say He is" said the Hindu to me, "but I must be reasonable. I am too little for His attention and not worthy of His love. I pray but I do not think He cares. I can only hope that my prayers have some influence on me or that they will reach some spirit, some ministering angels who will help me." "Christianity is a good religion for those who can believe it" said another, "but we Hindus are for the most part too intellectual to believe it. Life is not so simple and I am not so important."

Jesus confirmed His Gospel in many complicated life situations, and proved that God is always near and ready to reveal Himself to those who seek Him, and that the lowliest, most obscure and least worthy are important enough for the Father's loving attention.

Not only did Jesus confirm the Gospel, but He instructed His disciples to do the same, "As ye go preach, saying, 'the Kingdom of Heaven is at hand.' Heal the sick, cleanse the lepers, raise the dead, cast out devils." The disciples learned the lesson so well that Mark's Gospel tells us in its closing verse, "They went forth and preached everywhere, the Lord working with them and confirming the Word with signs following." Yet so little are these facts considered that it was possible for an eminent theologian to say publicly in this year, "The only task of the Church is to preach the Word." And some Missionary Societies appeal for support on the claim that all their resources are devoted to evangelistic preaching. The avowedly secular government of India may exert upon those Societies an influence that will promote the real mission of the Church through their reluctance to recognize Missions that only preach and run no schools, hospitals or other services to the needy.

The Confirmation of the Gospel

CHAPTER II

Confirmation Through the Healing Ministry

The Confirmation of the Gospel

The place of healing in the ministry of Jesus was large and central. We do not know how many people Jesus healed in the days when He dwelt in the flesh among men, but we do know that their number was legion. We do not know how much time He gave to healing, but in a full half of the chapters of the four Gospels there are records of Him healing the sick or the afflicted.

The Church through the centuries has always known that Jesus healed, but I find in the records of church history a surprising lack of consideration of why He healed. The Gospels make it clear that He not only made healing a large part of His ministry, but that He also commanded His disciples to give major attention to healing. Nevertheless, at times in church history the Church has seemed to be indifferent to health, and occasionally has even associated vigorous health with evil and physical weakness with holiness.

Some years ago there was considerable discussion in the Church in India of the reasons for the healing ministry. The issue was, do we heal people to make them Christians? Is the motive for medical missions, hospitals, dispensaries, public health activity and the healing ministry in all its forms the evangelistic motive? The conclusion reached in many church councils was that the Christian must minister to the sick because he is a Christian, and that he will suffer spiritual loss and be unfaithful to his Lord if he makes no effort to minister to the sick and the afflicted. I have strong sympathy with that conclusion, but it is not a complete statement of the case for healing. Jesus healed the sick because He was Jesus. It was His nature to heal. But His healing could not be separated from His evangelistic effort, for it proved the Gospel which He preached. He frankly pointed to His works of healing as a confirmation of His Gospel. St. Matthew tells us that Jesus stated, when He was healing a man sick with palsy, that He did so in order "that ye may know that the Son of Man hath power on earth to forgive sins." And the multitudes accepted this evidence as meaning what Jesus claimed that it meant, and immediately glorified God who had given the power that had been demonstrated so gloriously. Elsewhere, St. Matthew tells us that Jesus, in healing a man with a withered hand, claimed that His healing proved that His Gospel message was more authoritative than the law. "Is it lawful to heal on the Sabbath day?" asked those who cared naught for the sufferings of men, but much for the word of the law. And He answered them, "What man shall there be among you that shall have one sheep and if it fall into a pit on the Sabbath day will he not lay hold on it and lift it out? How much more is a man better than a sheep? Wherefore, it is lawful to do well (heal or meet any dire human need) on the Sabbath day." Then said He to the man, "Stretch forth thy hand. And he stretched it forth and it was restored whole like as the other."

When certain Pharisees belittled His healing and sought to explain it by an alliance with the Evil One, arguing that in healing the sick He was thwarting the will of God, who wanted them to suffer affliction, Jesus replied, "If I cast out devils by the power of Satan then is Satan divided against himself, and how shall his kingdom then stand? But if I cast out devils by the Spirit of God then the Kingdom of God is come unto you." To people who felt their privileged positions menaced, His message seemed not a Gospel but bad tidings, and His confirmation was not convincing. But where self-interest, falsely understood, did not close their minds to evidence, many people recognized the logic of His reasoning. It is true that they did not usually act upon that recognition. The false understanding by which they had judged Him was not completely removed by His reasoning or by the demonstration He made, but only those who saw some conflict between their self-interest and what He was saying and doing offered any objection to His statement.

In all His dealing with men Jesus refused to treat the sick, the lame, the deaf, the blind, the leprous, the weak as more sinful or less worthy than the well, the favored, or the mighty. Perhaps in treating men as equal before God, Jesus more forcefully challenged the prevailing philosophy than by anything that He said. He was thereby proclaiming, by the persuasiveness of action, that sickness is not ordained of God. It is astonishing that even after all that Jesus did and said about this matter, many who profess to be His disciples continue to regard sickness as an expression of God's will in relation to men. Who of us has not heard some sorrowful parent of an afflicted child say, "We must accept God's will?" Or who among us has not heard an effort to comfort bereaved persons by reference to the will of God being revealed in the death of a loved one? It is a libel on the character of God to suppose that it is His will that an innocent baby should be deprived of life, that a workman needed by his wife and children should be crushed to death because of a mechanical failure or a man's carelessness, or that a mother should spend her life on the ragged edge of nervous exhaustion. Jesus said, "I came to bring life and abundance of life" and He proved it in multitudinous instances by removing the obstacles to abundant living.

If God really wanted people to be sick and miserable Jesus would not have gone around healing them. On the contrary, He would have made the well sick, and epidemics would have broken out wherever He went. If God were such as many people believe Him to be, or such as even Christian ministers make Him out to be in such comments as those to which we have referred, He would certainly not have honored the calls of Jesus upon Him to heal. But because He is the loving Father whom Jesus proclaimed, interested in the welfare of all His children and eager to be recognized by them as seeking only their good, He did answer the calls of Jesus and His power met every kind of need for healing.

The concept that afflictions are a just punishment for sin has proved a powerful deterrent to medical practice. When the modern Christian missionary movement began in India, there were many goshalas (homes for sick and aged cows) in that country, but no hospitals for people, and medical science had stagnated completely. The philosophical Hindu had developed the theory of wrong behavior as the root cause of human troubles far beyond the place reached by the Jews. He had assumed as a fact a long succession of lives in order to account for ills and handicaps experienced from birth. Even the great Gandhi (to whom I cannot make even a passing reference without paying respect to his nobility of soul displayed supremely in the closing weeks of his life), in the early days of his dominance in India, denounced medical practice as an interference with God's plan of punishment and an encouragement to wrongdoing. The influence of Jesus, through the expanding knowledge of the Bible and the work of the Church united with the cumulative good effects of modern medicine, is forcing a change in the attitude of thoughtful Hindus, so that well-trained and competent medical practitioners are increasing in number rapidly, and the demand for their services is growing apace. Many generous gifts are being made to promote the public welfare through hospitals, sanatoria, clinics and preventive services. A few months before his death, one of Mahatma Gandhi's closest associates, the able and devoted Christian woman, Rajkumari Amrit Kaur, became, with his approval, the Minister of Health in independent India's first national cabinet. But one still hears from orthodox Hindus objections on religious grounds to the healing of the sick. When I suggested to a very wealthy Hindu of the conservative merchant class that he make a donation to a hospital in which Christian doctors were making a notable record of healing, he demurred, replying, "Who am I to interfere with God's purposes? If a man is both sick and poor it is proof that he is a sinner whom God is determined to punish. Had he sinned less he might have become ill, but he would have been able to pay for a doctor's services."

We ought to consider more than we are doing today, and more than the Church seemingly ever has done since the time of the apostles, the meaning of the commands Jesus repeatedly gave to His disciples to heal the sick. He made His ministry of preaching, teaching and healing the model which He commanded His disciples to adopt as their own. He told them to do whatsoever things they had seen Him do. He pointed out the multitudes that flocked to Him from the villages of Galilee and said to the disciples, in effect, "See how many there are who need to be helped. Helping them proves what I have been preaching about God. Many others should be doing this work. Pray that God may send others to do it." He likened the work that had to be done to the reaping of a harvest, bringing souls to God and said, "Pray the Lord of the harvest that He may send forth laborers into the harvest."

It is significant that this happened in villages in Galilee where these disciples lived. They knew these villages, they had been in them often, but they had never known the needs of the people as they saw them being revealed to Jesus. As long as people understood that God willed that they suffer, many of them endured their afflictions in silence and hid them from the eyes of their neighbors. Now they revealed them when they believed they could be cured. If God did not mean for them to suffer such handicaps, there was hope for them to be healed. They did not need to hide what could be removed. Because the disciples were with Jesus they saw human needs as they had never seen them before.

We today can live in any community, almost anywhere in the world, and be quite unaware of much of the suffering around us. Before the terrible disturbances that followed the partition of India, I had lived in Delhi for two and a half years. I had seen much of the Muslims of the city, but when the disturbances came I learned that I had known very little about their troubles. When hate-crazed Sikhs who had fled for their lives from Pakistan, leaving many of their relatives and neighbors dead at Muslim hands, attacked Delhi Muslims in retaliation, Mrs. Pickett and I worked with hundreds of other Christians and with the government to collect Muslims in refugee camps and care for them. Hundreds were brought in wounded, thousands with no possessions but the clothes on their backs. We were shocked by what we learned then of the chronic poverty of these people, of their physical handicaps and emaciation. This calamity had drawn the curtains aside so we could see our neighbors as they were and know how cruel life had been to them, when we had supposed that they were getting on at least moderately well.

Jesus has always wanted His disciples to see others as they really are, to see the shame and sorrow and suffering behind the curtains, and to proclaim and confirm the Gospel of God's enduring love for all men.

The evangelists do not tell us explicitly what the disciples did when Jesus showed them how needy people are and asked them to pray for laborers who would minister unto them, but they must have prayed, for it is recorded that a little later Jesus sent them out with definite instructions to do just what He had been doing, that is, to preach the Gospel that the Kingdom of Heaven is at hand (within quick reach of all), and to prove it by healing all manner of diseases. This was in the early stages of their training, but they had been so influenced by Jesus that they did as He told them. They preached and they healed.

At this stage in their training the disciples were directed to go only to people of their own race. They had not yet learned the Gospel well enough to apply it in their thinking or to proclaim it to people of other races, nor had their hearts grown large enough and Christian enough to heal the sickness of people with whom they had developed no community of interest, no sense of oneness. The order to go into all the world and preach and confirm the Gospel to every creature did not come until very near the close of their training, and was then accompanied by their Lord's promise to go with them everywhere. No such promise was given when first they were sent to their own people in Galilee. At that time Jesus shared the limitations that are common to all flesh. He could be only in one place at one time. After the disciples had acquired some experience in preaching and healing He told them, "He that believeth on Me, the works that I do shall he do also; and greater works than these shall he do; because I go to my Father." Going to the Father He would be freed from imprisonment in time and space, and would be able to go with them and work with them and through them. So it was that after the Resurrection He said unto them, "All power is given unto me in Heaven and in earth. Go ye, therefore and teach all nations… and lo! I am with you always, even unto the end of the world." Fortified by that promise, the disciples went forth preaching the Gospel with assurance, and confirming what they preached with the same miracles of healing that had helped to convince them of the Word of the Lord.

As a young man I had much difficulty over the promise that "greater works than these shall ye do." I could not believe that it would be possible for the disciples to do greater works than Jesus had done. But then I had not recognized the significance of the clause, "because I go to my Father." But the years I have spent as a missionary in India have removed this difficulty. I understand now how the disciples of Jesus can do greater works. I have seen them doing these greater works. Yes, I say humbly that I, even I, have participated in doing these greater works.

Jesus healed a number of sufferers from the foul disease of leprosy. We do not know how many He healed for Jesus never appointed a statistical secretary. He may have healed a hundred lepers. But His disciples are now healing thousands. It is probable that more lepers are being healed in India alone every month by His disciples in His name than Jesus Himself healed in His entire ministry in Galilee and Judaea. I think of a man whose ancestors were among the Outcastes of Hinduism. He was born an Outcaste. His father became a Christian when he was a small boy and put him into a Christian boarding school. Gifts made by disciples of Jesus living thousands of miles distant, who had never seen him or his homeland, made it possible for him to get an education. Faithful British and American missionaries and devoted Indian ministers and teachers helped him to become a fervent disciple of Jesus. Now he is a well-trained doctor, giving himself heroically to caring for leprosy sufferers. One hundred and thirty sufferers from leprosy are under his care. Many have been discharged from the Asylum as cured. Hundreds who have never left their homes have been treated in a network of clinics started by his initiative and operated under his direction, and have been healed without ever having suffered the humiliation of being branded as "lepers" or the devastation of being separated from home and loved ones.

In another institution, on one day I gave certificates to one hundred and six persons, saying that they had undergone prolonged treatment and were now free from discoverable evidence of leprosy infection. All over the world sufferers from this dread disease are being lovingly cared for by disciples of Jesus. This is the least imitated work of Christian Missions. Unless one has been deeply influenced by Jesus he will not undertake this work, or if he undertakes it he will soon give it up. Such is the record. Little service for sufferers from leprosy has been attempted anywhere until some disciple of Jesus has come among them to preach and prove His Gospel.

Jesus restored sight to a number of blinded eyes. The evangelists do not tell us how many. Again we notice the absence of a statistical secretary. It may be that fifty had their sight restored by His mercy. Perhaps the number was a hundred or even two hundred. But in restoring sight to blinded eyes, those who believe on Jesus are doing far greater works today. One British missionary friend of mine restored sight to over five thousand blinded eyes. An Indian Christian doctor, who but for Christ would have remained like his father and forefathers a despised, oppressed, illiterate, ill-nourished Outcaste, has removed hundreds of cataracts, sometimes twenty-five of them in one day. In a city of North India a Hindu doctor has developed an Eye Hospital in which many thousands have had their sight restored by skillful surgery, informed, up-to-date medicine and loving nursing care. At a recent public meeting in the presence of many Hindus he testified that, although he was not a professed Christian, the inspiration for all that he had done came from reading the New Testament and studying the work of Christian doctors and nurses. He added, "I believe that God is like Jesus and that to please Him we must serve like Jesus served."

The Confirmation of the Gospel

A strange perverseness is that which makes some disciples of Jesus deny the spiritual validity of all healing except what they label "faith cures." A truer instinct has led the Church to call Jesus "The Great Physician." The emphasis in the ministry of Jesus was on the healing and not on the method of healing. Just what His method was in most cases we do not know. It is important that we know that He healed, not how He healed. When Jesus commanded His disciples to heal He did not limit them to one method or warn them against medicines. By creating interest in healing, and disproving erroneous interpretation of the meaning of sickness that made people tolerant of others' suffering, Jesus gave the greatest impetus in human history to the science and art of healing. To this day medical science has made little progress where men believe that God sends sickness as an expression of His wrath, or where a fatalistic philosophy rules their minds. But wherever the disciples of Jesus have preached and confirmed the Gospel by healing, men and governments have become interested in sick people and so in medical science.

A young doctor of Pakistan who calls himself a Muslim told me, "Until I studied the Bible in a Christian college, I wanted to be educated only that I might earn much money and become rich and important. But when I read of what Jesus did for the sick and needy, I decided to study medicine and become a doctor." And then he added, "I know many Muslim doctors who are working to become rich; and a few who try to help people. All the latter have been influenced by Jesus." In an Indian Parsee doctor's office hangs a picture of Christ. He often points to it and says, "The good physicians all draw their inspiration from Him."

In refugee camps around Delhi during the terrible troubles of 1947, there were more than a hundred and forty thousand Muslims, driven from their homes, destitute, many of them wounded and sick. Cholera broke out. Heavy rains came and flooded the camp. Christian men and women, Indian, European, and American, worked heroically caring for the sick, dressing wounds, bringing in and distributing food and medicine and organizing and enforcing sanitation. Scores died daily and graves had to be dug. Among the refugees three Muslim doctors and several midwives were discovered doing nothing. Their co-religionists were suffering and dying, but they were doing nothing to help. I reproached them and pled with them but could get almost no service out of any of them, while Christian doctors were working to the point of exhaustion and collapse. Why? One of the doctors gave the answer. "Whatever is to be will be. Why should I interfere? I don't believe what you Christians believe and have no obligation to help in what you are doing." Most of the Muslims, while grateful for the help the Christians were giving them, gave no indication that their thinking about religion was in any way affected, but a few were heard to say, "These Christians practice what they preach." And one prominent Muslim business man said quite openly to a Christian minister, "We must revise our thinking about Christianity. What you Christians have done for us makes me love Christ. Perhaps, I, too, will be a Christian."

The essence of Islam's teaching is submission or resignation to the will of God. Alas! That will is misunderstood because the Gospel message about the character of God has been rejected by many generations of Muslims, or never heard with understanding. Preaching, teaching and healing, closely associated as in the ministry of Jesus, are necessary to the conversion of Muslims. The disillusioned, discouraged Muslims of today's India are probably the most accessible body of Muslims of comparable size in the world for those disciples of Jesus who are prepared to give a ministry modelled after that of our Lord, a ministry that preaches the Word persuasively and confirms it convincingly. The fatalism that lies at the center of Islamic thinking makes the concept of resignation or submission to the will of God logically inescapable. It is in complete contrast to the dynamism in the teaching and ministry of Jesus and to the dynamic service Jesus instructed His disciples to render. Here in the beautiful vale of Kashmir, where I am revising this manuscript for publication, a Muslim asked, "Sahib, why do people of other religions not serve the sick and needy like Christians do? Why do our Muslim teachers and preachers do none of those things which you missionaries of Christ do?" I replied that neither does the Muslim concept of God nor the example of Mohammed stimulate service. Unless associated with the conviction that God loves all men and seeks their highest good, religion produces no urge to serve. Islam has no Gospel for the healing ministry to confirm. When a Muslim or a Hindu serves the needy the stimulus comes from some source other than his religion, most frequently from influence exercised upon him directly or indirectly by Christ and His Church.

No confirmation or combination of confirmations of the Gospel will induce everyone to accept Jesus as Lord and Savior. St. Matthew tells us that when Jesus had healed two blind men, and made a dumb man to speak, the multitudes marveled and said, "It was never so seen in Israel." The Pharisees, beneficiaries of the status quo, refused to be convinced and accused Jesus of casting out devils through the prince of the devils. When Jesus first sent His disciples out to preach and heal He warned them to expect persecution and to be driven from city to city. "If they have called the master of the house of Beelzebub, how much more shall they call them of his household?"

The healing of the sick by the disciple of Christ in today's India is appreciated by many but discredited also by a number. "Exploitation of the people's diseases," "taking advantage of physical weakness to impose a foreign faith," and "proselytization at its worst" are some phrases opponents have used to discredit the healing ministry of the Church. If it is assumed in advance that the Christian Gospel is evil and that its acceptance by the populace will produce evil results, those who make such assumptions are likely to believe that their selfish interests or the interests of their order will suffer, and they are likely to attack the evidence that confirms the Gospel. Those Jews of Thessalonica who "took unto themselves certain lewd fellows of the baser sort" and "set all the city on an uproar," crying "these that have turned the world upside down are come here also," were in no mood to hear the Gospel or to consider evidence in its favor, for they assumed in advance that its acceptance by the people would adversely affect their position. So it was that Demetrius and his fellow silver-smiths would not hear the Gospel or allow the works that would confirm it to be done in their part of Asia by St. Paul. It is not necessary to consider all who oppose the preaching of the Gospel, and discredit the evidence that confirms it, as evil men. Demetrius was a man with influence among the silver-smiths, probably based upon a record of concern for their common welfare. The Pharisees who discredited Jesus and His works were in some respects the best element in the population of Galilee and Judaea. Among the Hindus and Muslims who reject the Gospel and discredit the work of the Hospitals, Sanatoria, and Leper Asylums are some who are acting from motives that are not entirely selfish or base. The Church must not develop a sense of antagonism to them but must patiently seek ways to continue its service, and endeavor, both by its work and the character it reveals to its opponents, to add confirmation to confirmation until the victory is won.

CHAPTER III

Confirmation Through Changed Lives

There is a way of confirming the incredible Gospel that is even more convincing than the healing of bodily afflictions. It is the remaking of men, the transforming of their characters and the enriching of their personalities. Jesus made abundant use of this method in the days when He walked among men in Galilee and Judaea. In this confirmation of the Gospel we find the most distinctive and most convincing of the miracles of Jesus. To it He gave even more of His time than He did to the meeting of physical needs.

Let us look at Jesus selecting His disciples, those in whom He was to perform the work that would prove His Gospel completely to far more people than His miracles of physical healing could ever reach. It seems that Jesus made these choices with deliberate purpose from among the most common and ordinary people about Him. St. Paul had some such thought in mind when he wrote, "We have this treasure in earthen vessels that the glory may be of God and not of men."

Great modern corporations with far reaching plans go to universities, and with the aid of psychologists and elaborate tests of aptitudes choose those who will represent them in handling their business. But Jesus, with a program more difficult than any corporation has ever adopted, went not to the learned or the mighty, and sought not those who would be accepted by their fellows as natural and inevitable leaders, but rather approached those who were without influence or apparent ability to develop influence – men who in every sense appeared ordinary – and then proceeded to demonstrate in them the transforming power of the truth which He had come to make known to men. He challenged the ideas that had depressed and weakened their personalities. In conversation, in the fellowship of worship and of daily life, in all manner of situations, He worked in them the liberating and energizing processes that prove the great affirmations of the Gospel. Radical change resulted. These men became living proof of the truth that Jesus taught.

Take Thomas. He was slow to believe, but Jesus developed within him such capacity for faith that he cried out, "My Lord and my God," and, if traditions that are implicitly believed by hundreds of thousands of Christians of Southern India be true, he became the most intrepid of all the apostles, journeying farther than did any other of them in obedience to the command to "go into all the world and preach the Gospel."

Take the impetuous but cowardly Simon. Jesus changed him into a disciple so steady that his very name was changed to Peter, the Rock, and he became so fearless and heroic that no hostile mob and no mighty ruler could control or even restrain him.

Take the ambitious sons of Zebedee. They were so reconstructed by Jesus that personal, selfish ambition ceased to characterize them and history knows them for their selfless devotion to the Savior. Whereas they had sought to be counted among the most important of disciples, when first they travelled with Jesus, His transforming grace made them willing to sacrifice all that they had, were and hoped to be that the truth might be known everywhere and the Church of their Lord be established in all the world.

The works of Jesus would have been forgotten long ago but for their significance in relation to the Word that He preached. The disciples who followed Jesus for His works' sake and did not understand that His works proved His Gospel, who saw no relation between what He said and what He did, left Him when

He gave His first clear affirmation of His Divine nature. None of them left a record of His wonderful works, and they seem to have returned, all of them, unchanged, to their ordinariness and obscurity. We do not even know the name of any one of them. But Peter exclaimed, "Thou hast the words of eternal life." He saw that the Gospel that Jesus preached was confirmed in His works, and that the works were significant chiefly because of what they proved. In our day men disparage words. "Mere words" is an oft-used expression. Who among us has not been foolish enough to use it? Yet words may be vastly important, and Peter was right! The final, most conclusive reason for following Jesus is the truth He preached, and the chief value of His marvelous works is that they prove His preaching. This understanding by Simon marked a stage in the process of change that made him a new man, a transformed man. He who recognized that the Gospel was proved by the healing ministry, became himself a proof of that Gospel by the change it wrought in him.

What one believes about God in relation to himself and others exercises a most potent effect upon his personality. I have seen amazing personality changes follow a change of faith. Men who had believed that God was against them because of their sins, which they were told that they had committed in earlier lives and who believed that God had caused men also to hold them in contempt, have come to know the Christian Gospel of God's infinitive love for them and have undergone a radical change in personality. From repressed and depressed individuals, they have changed into liberated and buoyant persons. Many have been saved from a sense of grievance and blessed with a sense of mission, saved from a fatalistic acquiescence in mediocrity or worse and blessed with an eager, determined purpose.

An old shoemaker who had accompanied Lord Roberts to Khandahar in Britain's war with Afghanistan and had come back to settle in his village, was so afflicted by his Hindu belief that his birth in an Untouchable home proved that God was angry with him, that his life became a misery. He had no strength with which to combat any hostile force in his life. His high-caste neighbors exploited him mercilessly and although he was resentful, he had no courage to defend himself. When an eye infection attacked him, he had no strength to throw it off and lost the use of one eye. His spirit was broken and even the smallest germs seemed to recognize that they had him at their mercy. But one day he met a Christian preacher, a man who, as a high-caste Hindu, had been an oppressive exploiter of such low-caste persons as he, and a drunkard, but had been completely transformed through faith in Christ. That preacher transmitted faith to him. The effect was amazing. Depression left him. Instead of gloom his face showed radiance. Instead of cowardice he manifested courage. He no longer thought of himself as a victim of the wrath of God, but as redeemed by the grace of God. His sense of grievance and helplessness left him and he developed a passion for service. His concept of God became that of his Heavenly Father, the tender, loving Father of all men, and he began to think of himself as the possessor of a treasure which he was called to share with his neighbors, a herald and pioneer of a new social order, the Kingdom of God. He became as impressively cheerful as he had been resentful and grouchy. He who had lived in fear of the police and habitually cringed before the servants of his land-owning neighbors, now fearlessly preached to all that Jesus is necessary for their salvation, and that through faith in Him they might obtain release from sin, as he had already obtained. The old shoemaker attended service a number of times in his own village or elsewhere when I preached, and I believe that everybody in the audience on those occasions was conscious of his presence, for his personality was charged with power. At times he could not contain his joy and shouted the praise of God.

At the heart of the Gospel is assurance that sins can be forgiven. The effect of that assurance on personality can be revolutionary. In a village in Bihar, which some regard as the citadel of Hindu orthodoxy, there lived a member of a criminal tribe. His ancestors for many generations had been renowned thieves. They developed certain techniques of entry to houses, and of removing possessions from houses and from the person of their victims, that probably have not been improved upon by any criminals anywhere. This man was taught by his own father, so that when a lad of ten he was an expert in several kinds of stealing. Then through the perfidy of men of his own tribe, who saved themselves from arrest by exposing him, he went to prison. After several prison sentences he met a preacher. He was at that time broken in spirit, convinced that the police knew him so well, and would watch him so closely, that he could never again steal without being caught, and yet equally convinced that there was no future for him except in crime. This preacher amazed him by telling him that he could be made as honest as the most honest man he had ever seen, that God could and would, if allowed, change him into a thoroughly worthy man and establish him in the confidence of his fellows so that he would not need to steal, nor need to be afraid of the wrath of men. When first he heard this Gospel he treated it as a good joke. He laughed that anyone would believe such nonsense, but in time the preacher convinced him that he at least believed what he said. Slowly this preacher led him to wish that this teaching might be true, and at last to believe that it was true. He accepted the good news by faith and there came upon him such power that his character was completely changed. People who had been afraid of him began to like him and to ask what had happened to him. Inside of two years the police released him from all supervision and showed their confidence in him. He was a changed man, a converted man, a man to whom the power had been given to become a child of God.

Saul of Tarsus, the self-righteous Hebrew bigot, persecutor of the Church, proved the Gospel when he was transformed into the humble devotee of Christ, the ardent evangelist, the most abundant in labor of all the ministers of Christ. So did Gulam Qadir, who, after he had organized the bad boys of his neighborhood to break up evangelistic services and tear up Bibles and Gospel portions, was so moved by the patient kindness of the preachers and colporteurs that he bought a New Testament, read the Gospel, was converted, and became such a zealous preacher that he was twice beaten severely, yet persisted and has brought hundreds to faith.

An illiterate but high-caste North India villager proved the Gospel when, hearing it for the first time from the lips of an itinerant American missionary, left father, mother, home and friends for Christ's sake and founded one of the most distinguished Christian families in North India. In the next generation that family consisted of an educator whose merits led to her appointment as Inspectress of Schools, a Rani whose witness to Christ by word and deeds of benevolence helped hundreds, a son who became the Chief Justice of the Chief Court of Oudh and retired with an unsullied record of probity, and two sons who rose to be District Magistrates and today in retirement serve their country as they did in active service, as exemplars of the good life and the Church as loyal and zealous laymen.

Rajah Sir Harnam Singh proved it when he gave up the throne of the rich state of Kapurthala, married the humble daughter of the minister who led him to Christ, and lived so much in the grace and fellowship of Jesus that he became one of India's most honored elder statesmen and the lay moderator of his church. One of his sons is Rajah Sir Maharaj Singh, whose ability and character led the cabinet of Jawaharlal Nehru to cross party lines to appoint him the first Governor, after Independence, of the large and difficult Province of Bombay. One of his first acts as Governor was the announcement that no alcoholic liquors would be served at Government House during his administration. The only daughter of Rajah Sir Harnam Singh is Rajkumari (Princess) Amrit Kaur, Minister of Health in Nehru's cabinet. She was one of Mr. Gandhi's closest associates and most trusted advisers during his long fight for Independence, and was an obvious choice for the ministry she now holds with eminent satisfaction to the nation. Her constant and passionate concern for the needy is recognized by all who know her. She is the most authoritative exponent of Mr. Gandhi's philosophy in or out of the cabinet, a statesman of the first rank and by the test of the people's respect, confidence and love deserves to be known as "The First Lady of India." A few weeks ago I asked how she and her brothers (all six of them have been eminent men) felt about their father's conversion and consequent loss of the throne. She replied, "We are profoundly grateful that he became a Christian and was removed from the succession to ruling power. These events and the example of service to God and man which our parents set for us saved us from becoming social parasites and selfish, ignorant exploiters of our countrymen." A prominent member of the Sikh community from which Harnam Singh emerged said to me, "Give us a few more Christian families like that of Rajah Sir Harnam Singh and all India will confess that Christ is Lord."

In India and Pakistan, far more than in the West, the individual is subject to group control. He does not ordinarily believe in his personal competence or ethical right to make important decisions in the realm of religious affiliation. Therefore, a demonstration of moral transformation and personality enrichment in a family is more effective than in an individual. And when the life of a community shows radical change for the better, the influence is most powerful. Fortunately the Gospel is being gloriously confirmed today in the life of many groups both in India and Pakistan. In the days of Bishops James M. Thoburn and Edwin W. Parker, in the last quarter of the nineteenth century, a revival movement of great power brought into the Church in the North India conference some thousands of people known as Mazhabi Sikhs. They were a depressed class people noted for crimes of violence. They had frequently revolted against the oppression of their overlords, and were kept under constant police surveillance. When the missionaries went to them with the Gospel they responded quickly, more, no doubt, from appreciation of the missionaries' interest in them than from conviction of the truth of what they preached. The higher castes were amused and rather pleased to have these criminals profess the Christian faith. Some said, "Now we need have no fear of Christianity. It will never amount to anything here, since these foolish missionaries have made our criminals the pioneers of the Church." But they knew naught of the power of Christ to regenerate. Within a dozen years these converted Mazhabis had been so redeemed and transformed that the police released them from special supervision and restored their civil rights. They were desperately poor, illiterate, despised and oppressed. But they sent their children to school, forsook idolatry and alcohol, and became industrious and peace-loving. Today few of their descendants show any recognizable sign of their depressed class origin. With few exceptions they have become firmly established in the Church and have won the respect of all classes. They have, to a large extent, conquered poverty and are well represented in the learned professions of medicine, teaching and law, in government service, and in the ministry of the Word and the Sacraments. But this process in North India is known by few in its entirety, because former Mazhabi Sikhs have left the villages where their former status was known and now are scattered widely through the cities and towns of India and Pakistan.

More effective, because better known and more clearly seen, group confirmations of the Gospel have occurred in what is now the Punjab of Western Pakistan, in Assam in the east, and in Andra-Desh and Tamilnad in the South of India. I can refer to only two of those groups. A poor, lame Untouchable in the Sialkot District of the Punjab led a movement that has brought more than four hundred thousand of his fellows to avowed Christian Faith and purpose. They are surrounded now exclusively by Muslims, but before the partition of India their neighbors included also many Hindus and Sikhs. Some years ago I spent a month among them collecting hard, factual data about changes that had taken place in them and among them subsequent to their conversion. The evidence of radical group betterment was overwhelming. Their neighbors of every creed and community testified that they were better, cleaner, and more intelligent than they had been. One Muslim said, "God has shown His love for them." A Hindu said, "I thank God for changing our worst enemies into our best friends." An old Sikh who fled from the Muslims and settled in a village in India where there are no Christians said recently, "We miss most of all in our new home the Christians whom we had seen rise from the depths to the heights of character. What we need now above all else is the salvation that came to them when they accepted Christ."

Many Hindu and Sikh neighbors of those converted Untouchables were saved by them from death at Muslim hands in the post-partition disturbances. In a public meeting recently held in India, a handsome Sikh retired official presided when a famous former Muslim, who is now a powerful Christian evangelist, preached Christ to a large audience of non-Christians. In the course of his address the evangelist expressed his gratitude that an eminent non-Christian was in the chair. At the close of the address the chairman corrected the preacher in these words, "I am not a non-Christian. I am known as a Sikh but I have accepted Jesus Christ as my Lord and Savior. In Pakistan I saw many Sikhs and Hindus killed but I prayed to Christ and He sent two of His disciples, former Untouchables, who at the risk of death to themselves and their families took me and my family to their homes, and then at night led us to safety. When we got into India, I went to a church and finding it locked, knelt on the steps and gave my heart to Jesus."

In Delhi, during these same disturbances when some Sikhs were threatening to kill Christians for saving the lives of Muslims, an elderly Sikh recognizing a Christian man in a crowded bazaar publicly embraced him and said, "Thank God for these heroic Christians! I am alive today because of them. They saved me from certain death in Pakistan. What if they also save Muslims here? Theirs is a religion of salvation."

In Andhra Desh in South India, I interviewed the Hindu caste leaders of a village about their Christian neighbors. As spokesmen those leaders chose two elderly brothers, who were prosperous farmers. The older, speaking first, said "These Christians were Untouchables and many were criminals. Their conversion made us very angry. We determined to treat them worse than ever. But they out-witted us. They became our best people. They had been very dirty, but are now very clean. They had been illiterate, irreligious, and stupid. Now they read more than any of us, hold church services every evening, and have become very intelligent. The difference between what they used to be and what they are now is the difference between the earth here and the sky there, between the darkness of midnight and the brightness of midday." The other brother broke in then with the statement, "We don't oppress them anymore. They are not Untouchables now. We admire them and even go to their church services. Someday we will all become Christians. Our Brahmans taught us that they were hopelessly evil and dirty and stupid. They wouldn't even let them come into our temples. Now we know that the Brahmans were wrong and in the future we'd rather be taught by these Christians than by the Brahmans."

The schools, especially boarding schools maintained by the Church, have an important place in the process by which transformation and enrichment comes to many individuals, families and communities who accept Christian faith and discipleship. Pupils who are committed to a confession of Christian faith, by their own decision or by family or community affiliation to the Church, provide an incomparably more fruitful field of service for Christian educators than do those who think of themselves as belonging to Hinduism or Islam and as under the necessity of being on guard against Christian indoctrination. And nothing is of more value to the Kingdom than to turn a nominal Christian youth into a radiant disciple of Jesus, trained in His teachings, bound to Him in love and worship, and experienced in His grace. While our Lord travelled widely, preached to vast multitudes and confirmed His preaching by His healing ministry everywhere He went, He nevertheless gave most of His time and attention to those whom He had enrolled in His School of Discipleship. It was through this school that He exercised the concentrated and continuous influence that radically remade the disciples. At their best, Boarding Schools conducted by able and consecrated Christians reproduce this transforming process. A boy from a family of newly-converted Outcastes brings to the School a personality already blighted and warped by the influences to which he and his family have been subjected in their hovel outside the village. He presents personality problems and needs that are much more complicated than those which Peter and his fellow disciples presented to Jesus. His youth, however, is an advantage. It makes responsiveness to Jesus easier.

A young boy, whose name for the sake of his children and other relatives I will not reveal, came to one of our schools from a family of Untouchables with a criminal background. They had recently professed Christian faith but continued to share all the disabilities which were imposed upon the community in which they lived. The boy had already been molded to the attitudes of the community, but before entering the school differed from his elders, chiefly in his eagerness to learn and become somebody. He was afraid of the higher castes who oppressed his people but did not, like his elders, think of lifelong submission to their oppression as inescapable. The Gospel had already given him hope of something better.

In school he quickly proved that he could learn and was not hopelessly stupid as he had often been told that he and all his people were. He also quickly dropped bad habits of speech and behavior and began to take on the ways of life that were taught by precept and example by his teachers, the matron in the hostel and by some of the older students whom he admired. He made steady progress and in due course finished high school and went to college, where he studied shorthand, typewriting, and bookkeeping. After two years in college he obtained employment in a government office. His efficiency, honesty, and courtesy won early and frequent promotion. He married a lady doctor who had emerged from a similar background, but was a generation removed from illiteracy and active oppression. They prospered abundantly and soon owned a lovely home and were on the road to wealth. But God called him to the ministry of preaching and her to the ministry of healing, and after some hesitation they responded and asked for and obtained an appointment to a locality in which there were no Christians, and had never been any preaching or witnessing to Christ. At the beginning of their work they were insulted and boycotted and had a very difficult time. Yet they established a church which, in less than a dozen years, grew to a membership of more than three thousand. He became a leading citizen of the Province, an honorary magistrate, a member of the legislature, a friend of the highest officials and a recognized spokesman for the weakest and most needy of the people.

In a small village in one of the most inaccessible areas of the Himalayan Mountains, a few families of Untouchables were converted. They were persecuted by the higher castes and by the unconverted majority of their own people. From among them a young boy went to a Boarding School in the civil and ecclesiastical headquarters of the District. In his own village he would not have been admitted to the school or the temple, being regarded as too stupid to learn, too degraded to associate with children of the privileged higher castes and inherently vicious. But he received instruction eagerly and responded with joy and developed mentally, spiritually, and physically. Soon he won recognition as one of the ablest students in the school where a large majority of the students were Brahman boys from homes of high privilege. That boy is today an eminent leader of the Church in North India, holds degrees from Indian and American

Universities, exercises a powerful influence for good in Church and State and confirms the Gospel in the beauty of his character, the richness of his personality and the Christ-like attitude he takes toward everyone he meets.

In all countries, round the world, wherever the Gospel is preached, there are some in whom the grace of God has wrought changes that confirm and commend the Gospel. The Church in every generation inherits the obligation to present this proof of the Gospel and can never limit its program to mere preaching without suffering disaster in its own life. Perhaps the most tragic fact about the Church of today is that among its members in every land are many who know nothing, by experience in their own lives or understanding observation in the lives of others, of this transformation of character and enrichment of personality that proves the Gospel. If this were not true and the Church were giving to the world through all of its members convincing evidence of the Truth of the Gospel it proclaims, its evangelistic successes would be far more numerous and mighty than they are now. Yet, as among those who heard Jesus preach and saw Him prove His Gospel, so now there would be some who would prefer darkness to light and would remain under the slavery of sin.

The Confirmation of the Gospel

CHAPTER IV

Confirmation Through the Resurrection

The Confirmation of the Gospel

The resurrection of Jesus from the dead was for Peter and his fellow disciples the supreme proof of the Gospel. This leader of the apostles indicated as much when he wrote in his first general epistle, "Blessed be the God and Father of our Lord Jesus Christ, which according to his abundant mercy hath begotten us again unto a lively hope by the resurrection of Jesus Christ from the dead." Despite all the evidence that Jesus had produced for them, they remained to some extent skeptical of the Gospel until He arose from the dead. Or perhaps it would be more accurate to say that the faith generated by earlier evidence was weak or ephemeral, and could not survive the tragedy of the crucifixion, death, and burial of Jesus. Then came the Resurrection and faith was reborn. After that instead of the tentative and hesitating acceptance of His teaching, there developed within them a strong and abiding conviction of its truthfulness.

Those first disciples were typical people and responded in a characteristically human way to the extraordinary. They followed Jesus faithfully, gave attention to what He said, and carefully watched His ministry. They wondered at His miracles of healing and at the change He effected in many minds and hearts. But the habits of thought and behavior which had formed before their association with Jesus began still held when they came to what apparently was the end of the road with Him. His arrest, trial, crucifixion, death, and burial left them bewildered and hopeless. They forsook Him in His hour of trial and looked upon all their past professions of faith as vain illusions. "We trusted that it had been He which should have redeemed Israel." Nothing less than this tremendous fact of the Resurrection could have revived their faith. Nothing less could have freed them from the inhibitions and conventions of the old life and made them new creatures in Christ.

I am acquainted with the questions some scholars have raised about the Resurrection of Jesus and do not regret them. No claim so stupendous and revolutionary should be accepted without the most careful examination of the facts. To make such a claim, or to teach that Jesus arose and ask people to believe it without offering evidence in confirmation, would be contrary to the procedure that Jesus always followed and that He taught His disciples to follow. The space at my disposal now will not allow a detailed examination of objections that have been raised or of the theories that have been evolved to account for the Resurrection. It is enough now to say that no credible explanation has been made or can be made of the change that came over the disciples apart from the proposition that Jesus did in very truth arise from the dead. At the time of crucifixion and immediately after it they were brokenhearted, defeated, frightened and divided. A few days later they were joyful, triumphant, courageous, and united. Had the records said nothing of the Resurrection, it would be necessary to postulate it to account for this change in the spirit and outlook of the disciples.

A humble Indian minister, with whom I had the joy of serving in the early days of my ministry, profoundly impressed me when, in my presence, he once silenced a blatant critic of the resurrection by speaking somewhat as follows: "I do not ask you to believe in the Resurrection because I say it happened or because this best book in the world contains accounts of men who walked and talked with Jesus before and after it happened, but because there is no other way to explain the Church that we see at work in India and nearly everywhere else in the world. If those disciples who lost their leader when He was killed and buried did not find Him again, then tell me what happened to change them so completely? What turned their defeat into victory, their cowardice into courage and their weakness into strength?"

Had there been no Resurrection, there could have been no continuing church. Had Simon not learned that His Lord had risen from the dead, he would never have become Peter but would have remained the weak, craven, impetuous fisherman into whom he lapsed when his early faith let him. Had there been no new evidence of the authority and divine nature of their Lord, memory of the old days would not have revived the dead and abandoned faith of James and John and Matthew and Andrew and their associates who did not even follow afar off as Peter did when Jesus went to His death. Authoritative tradition tells us that each of these disciples triumphantly overcame incomparably more severe testing in the later years than that in which they failed completely before the Resurrection. What but the Resurrection could have given them the strength to accept martyrdom for Christ's sake? What but the Resurrection could have swept away all their doubts and revived and drawn together the shattered bits of their earlier thinking into an integrated and lively faith?

Let us try to look into the minds of that little group of chosen disciples as the records reveal them immediately after the crucifixion. They had been with Jesus for approximately three years and the store of memories they carried was extraordinarily rich. They had heard Him preach to the multitudes, argue with the Scribes, Pharisees and Sadducees, and expound the Gospel in the semi-privacy of the group. They had been with Him as He prayed and He had taught them how to pray. They had asked Him questions which He had answered freely. He had even dealt with the unvoiced questions which they had hardly formulated in their minds. They had witnessed innumerable healings and under His direction had even experimented successfully in healing. They had admired Him, revered Him, obeyed Him, and had promised to follow Him always. They had hoped that He might become King of Israel and appoint each of them to a responsible position in His Kingdom, but had been puzzled by His reluctance to assume temporal power. They were convinced that God was with Him and that He performed miracles by the power of God. They had even vaguely sensed His oneness with God, and in a tentative sort of way had worshiped Him. But one of their number had so completely lost faith in Him that he had joined his enemies and betrayed Him unto death. All of them had been sorely disappointed that He did not destroy His enemies or at least oppose and defeat their conspiracy to kill Him. He had told them that His Kingdom was not of this world, but they didn't understand its nature. They saw no reason why He should die, or what benefit could come to them or to others from His death. He had told them that He must die but they refused to believe it. They wanted Him to live and to rule. They wanted to live and rule with Him. They had no thought of dying for Him. But they saw Him arrested. They knew that He was tried and made no defense of Himself. And then came the end, the crucifixion, His death and burial. Their hopes were destroyed. He was not the Son of God, not the Messiah, not the one for whom they looked, not the one who would redeem Israel. They had been mistaken, the Gospel was not confirmed, it was disproved. They would go back to their homes and try to forget it all.

Then came an unbelievable report that Jesus was alive again. What nonsense! The dead do not live again, not on this Earth! Who was responsible for this story? A woman, Mary Magdalene! She was not to be believed! She had an unsavory past and was always emotional. But what was this? The tomb was empty? Who said so? Mary the Magdalene and Joanna and Mary the mother of James? Well, what of it? Idle tales! But Peter, impetuous, as

The Confirmation of the Gospel

usual, decided to investigate. He ran to the sepulchre and found the linen clothes laid by themselves within the tomb and the body of Jesus gone. He didn't know what to make of it and departed wondering. Then came a report that two men, of their own number, had met Him on the road to Emmaus and had talked with Him. These men called the eleven together in Jerusalem and told them their experience, saying the Lord was risen indeed. And lo! Jesus stood in their midst. But they were slow to believe. Fright rather than faith possessed them. Jesus reproved them for being afraid and showed them His nail-pierced hands and feet as proof that it was He who stood before them. He confirmed the Resurrection and thereby confirmed His authority, His Divine nature and His Gospel. Their doubts left them forever. Henceforth they were witnesses for Him everywhere throughout their lives. No Judas emerged from among them after this, nor did any of them ever deny Him again.

In the latter part of the nineteenth century European skeptics claimed that there never had been a character such as Jesus, that the whole Gospel story was a myth that men had developed through a gradual process of addition and elaboration. That claim set scholars to a fresh study of the records and produced thereby such massive evidence of the historicity of Jesus that today no reputable student can be found anywhere who will dare question it. I am convinced that a scholarly study on the basis of modern psychological knowledge will produce, in time, equally impressive unanimity that the Resurrection occurred.

When I began my ministry in India, my bishop was Francis Wesley Warne, a man of apostolic devotion. On one occasion he was touring far back in the Himalayan Mountains when he met a priest of Hinduism, a Brahman who was greatly revered in his mountain community for his saintliness. Bishop Warne asked him if he knew anything about Christ and the old man said, "I have heard of Him from many people, have learned a little from this man and a little from that man, but I have never heard the whole story of His life. Please tell me all you know about Him." As Bishop Warne told the story of Jesus, from His birth through His ministry of wonderful works and great teaching to the crucifixion, he saw tears in the old priest's eyes, tears that a man who had done such wondrous things should be so cruelly put to death. Then the Bishop told of the Resurrection and the old priest first smiled with joy, then a look of fright came upon him and he said, "Is this so? Did this happen? Are you telling this story wherever you go?" And on hearing Bishop Warne's joyful affirmation, the old priest said, "Then get out of India! Stop telling this story! If the men of my country learn that such a thing as this happened, they will never again listen to sinners like me." The old priest recognized with an unerring instinct that the Resurrection is supreme proof of the Gospel, and that if men are thoroughly persuaded that such a one as Jesus was crucified and rose again they will turn from all the speculations and philosophies of men to this demonstration and confirmation of the Gospel, and recognize it as the central fact of history. Here is the proof of the Truth which, as St. Paul puts it, "makes all things consist," that gives meaning to life, that brings order out of chaos, that makes life a glorious adventure rather than a hopeless struggle that must end in defeat and destruction.

Many attempts have been made in this modern day to separate the indwelling Christ of the Epistles from the historic Jesus. One result of these attempts is an effort on the part of certain Hindus to equate the indwelling Christ with the spirit of the legendary heroes of Hinduism. The editor of a celebrated Indian weekly said to an American visitor a few years ago, "Your missionaries are unfortunately very little men. They insist upon preaching to India the historic Jesus who lived and died in Palestine. What they should do is preach a Cosmic Christ who came to the world in Ram, in Krishna, in Gautama the Buddha, in Moses, in Jesus and in Mohammed. The Hindu mind is too liberal to be impressed by so limited a presentation and interpretation as these little missionaries make." But when this visitor reported the Hindu editor's objections to a group of Indian Christians, a professor of philosophy in a governmental university aptly commented, "But who is it that rose from the dead? Who was it that convinced His disciples of His Divine character and mission? Who was it that did good to men and sent His disciples into the world to do good? Surely not Ram, not Krishna, not Gautama, not Mohammed, but only Jesus." What comparable confirmations of their teaching have any of the rivals of Jesus for the minds and hearts of men offered?

A sect of Muslims in Kashmir has counteracted the influence of the Resurrection upon those who know not the facts by claiming that Jesus only fainted on the cross and was revived by His disciples, and after being nursed back to strength went to Kashmir and died there. They show a grave which they declare to be His. No people present a more difficult task for the evangelist than do those Muslims who believe that Jesus is buried among them. On the other hand, nothing opens the heart to Jesus as does knowledge of the open tomb and our Lord's victory over death. The risen Lord alone can be the indwelling Christ, the Lord of Life, the Savior.

In Andhra Desh, the Telugu-speaking state of South India, there are more than a million non-Roman or Protestant Christians. It is the area of the largest and fastest-moving Christian mass movement. First the Untouchables, then the lower Sudras, fourth division of the recognized clean castes, and more recently upper class Sudras have turned to Christ in large numbers. One of the men who by their faith and zeal made these movements move was Venkayya, a converted robber chief. The story of Venkayya's conversion illustrates the power of the Resurrection as confirmation of the Gospel.

Venkayya and his fellow robbers terrorized a large population in a wide area. His only son, whom he loved dearly, fell ill. He asked certain priests of Hinduism to pray for his son's recovery. They exacted a very large fee which he paid from his ill-gotten gains. The son got worse. The priests demanded more money. Again, he paid. But the son died. He was grief stricken. For months he made no raids, but mourned for his son. Then a member of his band told him about a white man who was preaching a strange new religion at Bezwada. Venkayya listened with interest to all his fellow-robber told him and on the basis of what he heard composed a prayer. "O God, if Thou art, whoever Thou art, wherever Thou art, lead me to Thee." A year later he went to Bezwada to see the missionary and ask about the religion he was preaching. On the day of his arrival that missionary was utterly discouraged. The Brahmans, to whom he had been preaching on the river bank daily, had just told him to stop as they had heard enough and were no longer interested. This missionary, a Mr. Darling, had thought that sound strategy in missions called for the conversion of Brahmans first, as they were the natural leaders of the people. His plan had failed and God's plan he did not know. Venkayya began by telling him exactly who he and his six companions were. Somewhat doubtful, but knowing that he could not turn these bad men of the Untouchables away when they had come so far and under such hazards to hear the Gospel, the missionary told them the story of the birth of Jesus in a poor carpenter's home, of His wonderful works and teaching. As he reached the crucifixion, Venkayya leaped to his feet and said "Where are those evil men who killed Him? Tell us and we will destroy them." Mr. Darling explained that this had happened a long time ago in a distant country and that God had already dealt with the murderers. Then he told how Jesus arose from the dead. Venkayya again leaped to his feet and cried out, "Did it really happen? Is it true? Then He is my God. From this day I'll serve only Him." Venkayya was converted. So were his companions. They returned, disbanded the robber band and preached Christ to them. That was one of several notable conversions from which the great mass movement sprang. Venkayya became a preacher of the Gospel, and as long as he lived, even as a blind man in his old age, used the fact of the resurrection of Jesus as glorious confirmation of the Gospel. It would be difficult to say whether in that area it was the resurrection of Jesus or the transformation of the erstwhile robber chief into a saint of God that confirmed the Gospel most effectively. But certain it is that without the resurrection of Jesus there would have been no transformation of Venkayya.

On two days of the year, Christmas and Easter, the Churches of India with very rare exceptions are crowded to overflowing. If there is a church within a dozen miles and no conveyance is available, or he has no money to pay his fare, the poorest Christian will walk to join in worship on the days when the birth and the resurrection of Jesus are celebrated. Many non-Christians also go to church on Easter. More even than Christmas, the festival of Easter appeals to the Hindu mind. Every founder of a religion, every prophet, teacher or preacher was born somewhere on some day, but only Christ has risen from the dead. Ardent disciples of Mahatma Gandhi, professing to find a parallel in the lives of their master and our Lord, for some weeks hoped for a resurrection of Mr. Gandhi. Imagine the effect if the Mahatma had returned to life. How convincingly it would have confirmed in popular and learned thinking alike, the wisdom of his teachings and the goodness of his character! Mr. Gandhi has not risen again, nor has any other than Jesus, and His Resurrection remains for the thoughtful in every land a convincing confirmation of the truth He preached and of His Divine nature and mission.

St. Paul wrote of "knowing the power of His Resurrection." That power does many things for those who know it and admit it to their hearts and minds, and not the least of them is the complete removal of doubt and indecision in relation to Jesus. The Christian who does not believe in the Resurrection of Jesus misses from his life a power which contributed much to the winsomeness of St. Paul and to the success of his ministry. Is it not true that where this confirmation of the Gospel is rejected the Gospel seems to be believed only tentatively and weakly, or not at all, and that character and personality are seen to have missed the renewal and enrichment that acceptance of the fact of the resurrection brought to the early disciples? One occasionally meets Arya Samajists or the Brahma-Samajists who profess to believe in Jesus as an inspired teacher, a saint and even an incarnation of God but reject the resurrection. One quickly discovers that they likewise reject the central and distinctive teachings of Jesus about the character of God and with them the obligations of discipleship as Jesus expounded them.

Is it because the resurrection is the most convincing confirmation of the Gospel that some critics reserve it for their most severe criticism? It is when schools and hospitals lead to conversions that opposition to them arises. It is when converted Untouchables undergo radical transformation in character and become effective witnesses to the unique power of Christ that demands are made by some higher caste Hindus for interference by their leaders, or by the government, with Christian work for Untouchables.

Naturally it is when Christians demonstrate that they know Christ and the power of His Resurrection that objection is taken to the resurrection as fact.

CHAPTER V

Confirmation by the Holy Spirit

The Confirmation of the Gospel

Jesus promised a confirmation of His Gospel and Mission would be sent from Heaven after the withdrawal of His physical presence. "I will pray the Father, and He shall give you another Comforter, that He may abide with you forever; even the Spirit of Truth; whom the world cannot receive, because it seeth Him not, neither knoweth Him, but ye know Him, for He dwelleth with you, and shall be in you... The Comforter which is the Holy Ghost, whom the Father will send in my name, and He shall teach you all things and bring all things to remembrance whatsoever I have said unto you... He will guide you into all truth... He will glorify me."

This promise was fulfilled for the earliest disciples at Pentecost. But it was not cancelled with its first fulfillment. It has been fulfilled for an innumerable company of people in the subsequent years and may now be confidently interpreted as a promise to the Christians of every age and country.

The Muslims have taught that the promise was fulfilled in the coming of Mohammed and not before or since. But Mohammed did not prove to be a Comforter for Christ's people. He did not glorify Christ. He did not bring to remembrance what Jesus had said.

The Holy Spirit came upon those first believers and brought all that Jesus promised: comfort, remembrance, power, and guidance. And He remained with them comforting, reminding them of Jesus, empowering them for service and guiding them in further search for truth. There is no evidence that any of them ever again needed any new confirmation. They counted the Gospel proved beyond doubt or question. But many issues arose on which they needed instruction concerning the mind of Christ. What was it that He had said? What would He have them do?

Be it noted that the promise, "He shall teach you all things and bring all things to remembrance whatsoever I have taught you," was not given to one disciple separately or to a section of them, but to the whole group, and was accompanied by a plea that they accept jointly the responsibility that He had given them, and by a prayer to the Father that they might all be one, "As thou, Father, art in me, and I in thee, that they also may be one in us." If the Church is not today enriched with all spiritual knowledge and is unable to confirm for all men the Gospel as preached by Jesus, surely a sufficient reason is its divided state. When the disciples were one at Pentecost, their witness unto Christ immediately after the coming of the Holy Spirit upon them and within them was with such power and persuasiveness that about three thousand people were added unto the Church in one day. And after that, while their oneness was apparent, daily additions were made to the Church.

In India it has often happened that in an area of considerable size the Christians are all of one accord, and I have observed that earnest waiting on God under such conditions has brought results in spiritual power and appeal to non-Christians immeasurably greater than what has come from comparable effort in areas where Christians have been divided into competing sects. Where Christians united in faith and hope and love receive the Holy Spirit, they are comforted, instructed in Spiritual things, and empowered to win souls. I could tell you story after story of mighty ingatherings despite the fact that the union was only a restricted local one. What might not be expected by way of the response of the world to this confirmation by the Holy Spirit if the union of the Church were state-wide or nation-wide? On the other hand, there are many instances that show how evangelistic effectiveness has waned and disappeared when denominational competition, disputing over doctrine, or ambitious seeking for leadership have intervened.

In an area a short distance south of Calcutta over a hundred years ago a revival of remarkable power began through the work of several British missionaries. Three men were gloriously converted. With the missionaries who led them to Christ they waited on God until they received power. They became His witnesses and soon scores were converted, then hundreds and within a year two thousand. Tens of thousands became interested and it looked like the entire population of the area would turn to Christ. Then missionaries of another church came in and told the new converts that their ministers were not properly ordained. They divided the Church. Then another group of missionaries arrived and said that the converts in the area had not received the right kind of baptism. Then the Roman Catholics arrived and said that they alone were the true Church of Christ. The ingathering of converts stopped. The joy and power of the Church were lost. Spiritual decline set in. The area is today one of the most difficult in India.

A certain effectiveness displayed at times by sectarians in taking members away from older churches should not be mistaken for the sort of thing that happened at Pentecost. There is a vast difference between winning non-Christians to Christian discipleship and persuading disciples of Jesus to leave one denomination for another. The former surely strengthens; the latter may weaken the Church of Christ.

One of the most tragic aspects of the missionary movement of today is that many small sects are vigorously working to divide the Church in areas where the population is mainly non-Christian. Often this is done in the name of the Holy Spirit. Much of the energy of these sects is spent in fighting the existing Church and not in seeking the conversion of unbelievers. They profess the baptism of the Holy Spirit, but give no indication that there has been brought to remembrance in their minds the Lord's command about healing the sick or teaching, for they run no hospitals and no schools. Nor do they appear to give any consideration to our Lord's Prayer for the union of His disciples. It is significant that they have won few converts from the non-Christian people, even in those few areas into which they have gone for that purpose, and that a large proportion of those whom they entice away from other churches do not stay with them long.

Men who have received the Holy Spirit will ordinarily follow the method of the Master in preaching and confirming the Gospel. They will try to meet human need of every sort, healing the sick and the afflicted, comforting them that mourn, cleansing the lepers, teaching the ignorant and the misinformed, counseling the unwise and warning the sinful. They will try to live at peace with all men and especially with their brethren of the faith.

It is heartening that except for the groups mentioned above and the Roman Catholics, the Churches in India and Pakistan are seeking more and more earnestly to attain unto and demonstrate unity. Through comity agreements, union in educational institutions (including schools of theology), territorial demarcations, cooperation through Bible Societies, Tract Societies and Publishing Houses, simultaneous procedures in evangelism, attention to special needs, and negotiations for organic unity, they are reducing the losses to the Kingdom caused by their divisions and moving toward that blessed oneness which will fulfill their Lord's desire for them. I would use this occasion to appeal for union in western countries, which will remove the necessity of accomplishing union in India and Pakistan at the cost of separation in church membership from beloved Christian comrades in those countries. The call the Methodist bishops made in 1948 for a comprehensive union needs to be reiterated again and again until the response brings its glorious achievement.

The confirmation of the Gospel given by the Holy Spirit at Pentecost is a powerful demonstration of the meaning of the Gospel for a war-weary world. It showed the results of being of one accord in faith and brotherly love. These disciples were in a hostile world. The government was against them. The people were against them. They had gone through a very difficult time of being divided and discouraged. They had been guilty of disloyalty to their leader. But the Resurrection had brought them together again and restored their faith. They had repented and pledged themselves anew to Jesus Christ. They no longer felt guilty, and were not blaming one another. No one was seeking leadership. With one accord they prayed for the coming of the promised Comforter, Teacher and Guide. And He came with power. His presence not only confirmed the Gospel afresh and finally for every one of them, but made the onlookers sure that God was with them. Among those onlookers were men of many nations and tongues. Ordinarily they would not all be able to understand, but in this strange situation all understood what was going on. They knew that the Holy Spirit had come upon the disciples. The praise of God and the witness to Christ that issued from the lips of the Spirit-filled disciples was understood by every one of them as though spoken in his own language. The great trouble in the world of our day is that people do not understand one another. They speak different languages even when they use the same words. "Democracy," "imperialism," "communism," "America," and "Russia" take on different meanings as they are used by people of different backgrounds of experience and "indoctrination." A divided Church, lacking the guidance and empowerment that came at Pentecost when the Church was one, seems able to do little about it. Its witness is weak and ineffective. Even its vocabulary of religion is misunderstood. To so good a man as Mahatma Gandhi "conversion" suggested religious imperialism. "Jesus Christ, the son of God" shocks devout Muslims. A Pentecost experienced by a united Church is needed to convince the world of Christ and bring the nations to an appreciation of the meaning of the Kingdom of God. When that comes, a modern Peter will be able to talk again of Jesus of Nazareth as "a man approved of God among you by miracles and wonders and signs which God did by him in the midst of you, as ye yourselves also know," and again will be able to say, "Repent and be baptized every one of you in the name of Jesus Christ for the remission of sins and ye shall receive the gift of the Holy Ghost. For the promise is unto you and to your children and to all that are afar off."

Speaking with other tongues was an experience of great utilitarian value as it came to the disciples at Pentecost. It led to the conversion of many persons, who through it came to an understanding of the Gospel. But there is evidence in St. Paul's writings that some in the early church sought the experience as an emotional satisfaction without concern for others. That was condemned by St. Paul as lacking the authenticity of the Pentecostal experience and being for personal edification rather than for the good of others. Today, likewise, there are some who seek the gift of tongues for personal satisfaction without concern for its utilitarian value to the Church and in disregard of the essential condition of unity in the Church. For a real Pentecost that confirms the Gospel and convinces the unconverted so that they are brought to the Savior, unity is necessary and by it unity is promoted. But an imitation Pentecost, conceived in selfishness, divides and weakens the Church, and often repels and antagonizes unconverted onlookers.

In India now various groups are working under names suggestive of Pentecost as their special interest, such as the "Pentecostal Church of Christ," the "Pentecostal Holiness Church," and the "Pentecostal Assembly." It is sad to see how they misrepresent Pentecost and how far their achievements fall short of those of the disciples at the original Pentecost. Their influence seems to be completely divisive. I have never seen or heard of an instance where they have drawn the disciples of Christ together into a wider and richer fellowship, neither have I heard of one case where a non-Christian onlooker has come to Christian faith, experience, or purpose through understanding the "unknown" tongue in which they have spoken. On one occasion a Methodist missionary was assaulted by several enthusiastic "Pentecostalists" for expressing doubt that what he saw and heard was the real thing, and in several places Methodist and other churches have been disrupted by competing "Pentecostal churches" which ran in weakness a few years and died for lack of spiritual renewal. The only protection against this sort of counterfeit Pentecostalism is the development of the genuine experience that adds to fervent preaching the confirmations that Jesus provided and taught the Church to provide – the healing ministry, the teaching ministry, the transformation of character and enrichment of personality that result from a sustained personal work, joyful acceptance of the Resurrection, the unity of the Church and the genuine baptism of the Holy Spirit.

In his epistle to the Ephesians St. Paul writes of the seal of the Holy Spirit on them after they believed on Jesus. He saw the confirmation of the Holy Spirit as a seal that made further proof of the Gospel unnecessary. The author of the epistle to the Romans prays, "Now the God of hope fill you with all joy and peace in believing, that ye may abound in hope, through the power of the Holy Ghost." When the Christian has received the Holy Ghost (i.e. the Holy Spirit) he has joy and peace in believing, for his doubts leave him, and he abounds in hope. He is not pessimistic, he does not expect the worst, he faces the future in confidence. The Honorable C. Rajagopalachariar, the last Governor General of India, serving in the transition period between British rule and Independence, who resigned to make way for the first President of the Republic, addressing a body of Hindu business men a few months before he vacated his high office, pleaded for the conquest of pessimism and the determined cultivation of an attitude of hopefulness. He suggested that pessimism is a characteristic of the East. He would have been more accurate had he said that pessimism is characteristic of all non-Christian cultures. Hope is distinctly a Christian virtue. It is bracketed with faith and charity both by St. Paul and St. Peter. "We are saved by hope," says St. Paul. Hard factual data are available to prove that after final confirmation of the Gospel has been received through the baptism of the Holy Spirit the heart and mind of the established believer becomes optimistic, cheerful, expectant of good, abounding in hope. Again this author of the epistle to the Romans says, "For as many as are led by the Spirit of God, they are the sons of God" and "The Spirit itself bears witness with our spirit, that we are the children of God." The Holy Spirit not only confirms the Gospel as true, but confirms to the believer that this Gospel is working in him for his personal salvation.

On a railway train in India several years ago, I met an aged Muslim gentleman, who seeing me reading the Bible and learning that I was a Christian minister, said, "Tell me what you know about God. Don't tell me what you have read about Him, or have heard about

Him, but what you know. I am not interested in dogma." I replied, "Jesus taught us about God and proved what He taught. I know that what Jesus taught is true because He proved it thoroughly and promised the Holy Spirit to prove it again and again to those who wish to be taught. The Holy Spirit will prove it to you. You can know that God is love, that God hears prayer, that your sins are forgiven, that He is with you and in you, that He is your loving Heavenly Father and that Jesus Christ is your Lord and Savior. These things I know and you may know them." There were tears in his eyes as he answered, "I have been a faithful Muslim but I have no such knowledge as you mention. Pray for me." I prayed for him then and I have prayed for him often since. I have never met him again, but I hope he has come to faith and knowledge. The Holy Spirit was obviously working in his heart and was ready when he surrendered to bear witness to his spirit concerning the things of God.

The yearning for authoritative, decisive experience, while of varying degrees of intensity, is well nigh universal among men. Our Lord provided for its satisfaction. A Church ministering after the example of Jesus, obedient to His commands and responsive to His will, as revealed in His teaching and prayers, will produce that authoritative experience for which the heart longs. It is not to the Roman segment of His Church, pursuing policies that divide, confessing only the sins of others, proclaiming its own infallibility, persistently fighting against other Christians and rejecting all approaches toward unity, that yearning hearts can look for authoritative expositions. Millions outside of Roman fellowship have acquired the authoritative experience of a personal Pentecost, a gift of the Holy Spirit that has brought to them instruction, comfort, and conclusive confirmation of the Gospel. I think of many whom I have known in India and America in whom the

The Confirmation of the Gospel

Gospel has been so gloriously confirmed that they have walked in joy before the Lord all their days and have radiated proof of the Gospel. I think of Rev. C. M. Humphrey, an aged pastor in my boyhood days more than four decades ago; of my mother, Ludie Day Pickett, a saint for at least fifty years; of Caroline Mamma, physically infirm and spiritually robust in Lucknow when I began my ministry in 1910; of Rev. Mathew Stephen, converted from Muslim stock, serene and gracious amid the perplexing confusions of a difficult pastorate; of Ishwar Dayal, from a high-caste Hindu home, an ardent rural evangelist, who for Christ's sake entered into all the suffering and sorrow of the Untouchables to proclaim and demonstrate the abiding joy of conscious salvation. These, and many others in whom I have seen God at work, have passed beyond the stage when further confirmation of the Gospel was needed for them and so in God's hand they were made living confirmations of its truth and power.

A reporter for a daily newspaper published in the Hindi language came to me recently as an enquirer. He had for a dozen years been a member of a Hindu ascetic order. He said, "I have tried the prescriptions of my Hindu guru (teacher) and they do not work. My three brothers, knowing Hinduism as poor cultivators get to know it from the tyranny of the priests over them, have found it so disappointing that they have become Communists. I want to right the wrongs of the poor and oppressed in my country and what Communists promise to do for them arouses my enthusiasm. But I do not like the lawlessness of Communism, its preaching of hatred and murder. What little I know of Christianity appeals to me. I suspect that Christ would make a better Lord for me and for India than Stalin would. But how am I to know that this is so?" I gave him a New Testament and told him to give attention in reading to how Christ proved His Divine mission and message by outward signs and then open his mind and heart for the coming of the Holy Spirit that would convince him by an inner witness.

That young man is representative of a great company in India now. Dissatisfied with the teachings that have allowed ancient evils to afflict their people for uncounted centuries almost unchallenged, they yearn for a deliverance for themselves and their country. They are not disposed to accept any new teaching without question. They want proof. How fortunate that the Christian Gospel comes to them so richly confirmed and offers to all who will respond wholeheartedly the final confirmation of the Spirit's witness with their spirits!

CHAPTER VI

Confirmation Through the Church

The Confirmation of the Gospel

The universal relevancy and eternal urgency of the Gospel make its confirmation necessary day after day in innumerable places and conditions. Every individual everywhere is entitled in the plan of God both to hear the Gospel and to receive proof that it is true. Our Lord assigned to the Church the responsibility for implementing this plan of God. "Go ye, therefore, and teach all nations, baptizing them in the name of the Father and of the Son and of the Holy Ghost; teaching them to observe all things whatsoever I have commanded you: and lo, I am with you always, even unto the end of the world."

That commission is definite. The task it confers is comprehensive. No mere proclamation of the Gospel will suffice to teach all nations and bring them to conviction, confession, and baptism. Confirmation is essential. And the commission carries with it a clear promise of the presence of the Lord when the attempt for fulfillment is made.

When that commission is considered against the background of today's world, it can be seen that the need of the greatest urgency is to prove the relevancy and value of the Gospel for nations and the whole family of nations. It is frightful heresy to present the Gospel as intended only for individuals. Jesus preached good news for the individual and confirmed it in His dealing with many individuals, but He also preached the Gospel of the Kingdom. Kingdoms rule over nations. They deal with group life, with the relations of people to one another and with society as a whole. Jesus during His days in the flesh saved many individuals in Galilee and Judaea, both from their sins and the sins committed against them by other individuals, by society, and by the government, and He repeatedly called for a society that would not commit sins against the individual. He preached the Kingdom as the rule of the loving

Heavenly Father in the lives of men, and taught His disciples to pray for its coming when the will of God would be done on earth as it is in Heaven, when all men would have their daily bread and would forgive one another's trespasses as they hoped God would forgive theirs. He addressed much of His effort with His disciples to the task of forming them into a beloved community. He wanted them in their relations with one another to demonstrate what the rule of God in the lives of men would mean for the whole world. They were to preach to nations and to do before the nations what they had seen Him do. And while doing this, they were to have salt within themselves and live at peace one with another. They were to love one another as God had loved Him and He had loved them. He assured them that if they were united in love, men would recognize that what they preached was true and would accept Him.

The Church has confirmed the Gospel. Admittedly it has not at any time been all our Lord Jesus has called it to be, but it has been so superior to every human institution that it has given real evidence of its Divine origin, nature and mission, and of the fact that God is in it and working through it. The fact that the Church has survived is itself a confirmation of the Gospel. When we look at the little group of disciples just before and immediately after the crucifixion and note their weakness, disillusionment and divided state, we marvel that they could ever form the Church and undertake the immense task for which they had been trained and were soon to be commissioned. By any reasonable standard of human effort they could not be expected to reassemble, to say nothing of surviving as a group. Had they not been the Church, chosen by the Lord of the Church, they would have been scattered and their faith and fellowship, if not they themselves, utterly destroyed. Yet they are drawn together by the fact of the Resurrection, their faith and fellowship restored and confirmed forever, and they succeed in transmitting faith to many others and establishing them in the Church. The miracle-working Jesus fulfills His promise. He is with them again. It is remarkable that the new converts whom the disciples admitted to the Church held firm in faith and fellowship and purpose when the despotic government of the day and the false religious leaders of Judaism united to destroy them. It is remarkable that through fifty-eight successive generations the Church has been able to maintain and increase its strength by transmitting its faith to others and bringing them into the body of Christ. In that process terrific opposition has been met many times and the opposition has even invaded the Church.

I talked one day with a leader in the political life of one of India's great provinces. He belonged to a very able sub-caste of Brahmans. His ancestors for many generations had wielded power over their fellowmen. His mind was astute. He said, "We Brahmans have exercised power in India for thousands of years, but I now see that the end of our power is coming unless we come to terms with Jesus Christ and His Church." He went on to say that he was perplexed about the life of the Church. He had studied Church history, had learned of corrupt popes and bishops, of clergymen who suppressed the great affirmations of the Church concerning salvation through faith in Christ and made themselves arbiters of the soul's destiny, sold indulgences for sin and generally betrayed their professed Savior and Lord. "And yet," said he, "the Church lives. It can't be destroyed. Its life and growth are proof of the Gospel. We Brahmans must confess that Christ is Lord or the converted Untouchables will be the new leaders and teachers of India."

When the modern era of Christian missions began in India, good works were recognized by Hindus generally as worthwhile only because they enabled those performing them to acquire merit, which tended in a small way to offset the bad effects of evil deeds performed in many previous incarnations. The Hindu found it very difficult to imagine men caring to serve others outside of their home or community for any reason other than acquiring personal merit. But today so far has the Church modified that thinking that great numbers of Hindus are prepared to declare that the Church is a Divine society seeking the good of all men and not merely personal gain for its members. Some time ago I talked with a Brahman who has charge of a great temple and is the leader of a group of temple priests. He said to me, "We have many worshippers, but although we have a caste system these worshippers who come to the temple come with no sense of community. They come as individuals and have nothing like your Christian program of congregational worship. Our castes are social institutions, concerned entirely with human affairs in this life. Your Church is something other than that; it is a Divine institution. Your people believe in congregational prayer. Your people have tasks that belong to them together. They have a sense of community. We Hindus must develop something like it, but we don't know how to do it."

The history of Hinduism contains the records of many men and an occasional woman who developed great saintliness of character. But because there was no Divine society, little sense of unity, the faith of the individual was not frequently communicated to others and no great continuing redemptive movement ever developed in Hinduism. The Church, on the other hand, has been a continuing force for human redemption. The Church has possessed Christ, and His claims have been proved through its life.

One hundred forty years ago, a work of grace was begun in South India when God created in the heart of a very ordinary Outcaste of a village near the southernmost tip of India a great longing for some experience of Himself. This man, because he was an Outcaste by birth, was forbidden to enter any temple of Hinduism. He had heard stories of men who through worship in the temples had acquired a religious experience which made them happy and noble. He thought that if he could only get into one of the temples and stand or kneel before the idol he would find happiness and release from sin. So he resolved to leave home, go into areas where no one knew him and represent himself as a man of some higher caste in order that he might get into the temples. He did this, but in the temples he found so much of vice and evil of every sort that he was disillusioned. When he was about to give up the search for God altogether, and at a time when his heart was very sore about the injustice done to him and to the Outcastes generally, he heard of a certain temple four hundred miles away which was reputed to be especially sacred and where, it was said, many people had come to know God. He determined that he would go there also. There were then no trains and no cars, and he had no money with which to hire a horse or to travel any part of the way by any sort of conveyance, so he started out to walk. As he could afford to eat very little on the long pilgrimage, he became utterly weak and exhausted, but still pressed on and on and on. At last, barely able to walk, he arrived at his destination, stumbling into the precincts of the temple. But there he found vice more entrenched and more hideous than he had ever seen it. Prostitution was carried on openly in the temple and the priests shared the "earnings" of the poor girls. Throwing himself down in utter weariness and sick of soul, he dropped into a troubled sleep. In the early hours of the morning he had a mysterious experience in which a "voice" said to him, "Arise! Listen! You have wanted an experience of God. For a long time you have sought to know God. You have paid a great price for that privilege. You will not find Him here, but get up, start back home, and along the road you will meet one who will introduce you to God." He started home, his weariness miraculously taken from him. He had walked some three hundred miles on the return journey when to his surprise he met on the roadside a distant relative, who asked where he had been. He told him of his trip and his disappointment, and then of the Voice that promised him that he would meet one on the way home who would help him to know God. This relative's face shone with joy for he had a few weeks before found God. He said, "Come with me. I have found God. I will take you to one who will help you to find Him." And Vedamanickam, for such became his name, followed this distant kinsman to the home of a German missionary who told him at once of Christ. He believed and was gloriously converted. A few months later he was back in his own village preaching Christ and establishing the Church of Christ. The first to join him were members of his own family. They were followed by other Outcastes of the village. In the main these new converts were not good men. An early missionary who joined Vedamanickam a few months later said of them, after their number had increased to more than a thousand, "In the main these believers on Christ, who call themselves Christians, are rogues and scoundrels." Yet Christ was beginning a work in them through Vedamanickam that has made them a beloved community, a Divine society, a true Church that confirms the claims of Christ.

In that same area I spent a month studying these congregations which Vedamanickam founded. There I found that none in the surrounding community would think of using that frank early missionary's appellation, "rogues and scoundrels," for the descendants of Vedamanickam's converts. On the contrary, they were generally accepted by Hindus and Muslims as the best men and best women in those parts. Before the conversion of

Vedamanickam, his fellow caste-men, though not he himself, were all illiterate. One hundred twenty five years later the descendants of those early converts, with others who had joined the Church from among the Untouchables, were running the schools of the whole area and the former Brahman teachers were sending their own sons and daughters to their schools. When Vedamanickam was converted, his caste fellows followed in the main the occupation of drawing toddy from the palm trees, fermenting it and selling it, and supplementing their income from this source by performing menial tasks of the baser sorts, for which they were paid the most meager wages. But at the time of my visit the Christians were not at all represented among liquor dealers and few of them did any of the so-called "menial" jobs. They were respected leaders of the community, the most progressive and constructive element in the life of their villages. In a wide area around that village where Vedamanickam lived and preached Christ, I found no Brahman priests. When I asked the people why that was so, they replied, "We got tired of them. They had exploited us and our forefathers a long time, choosing auspicious days, lording it over us, telling us what we could do and when we could do it, and they never did anything of real value. On the other hand, we saw the Christian preachers and what they did for the Church. We saw them visiting the homes of their people in times of sickness, gathering the children together to teach them, opening and maintaining schools and dispensaries, and we said 'Unless our priests can change and become like unto those preachers we don't want them here.' They wouldn't change so we drove them away."

The Church was made to be one. The fact that it is not one undoubtedly limits the extent to which it can convince the world of the truth of the Gospel. Jesus said to His disciples that if the world would see that they were one it would believe on Him. It is surprising that people who profess the utmost devotion to Jesus are so often totally unconcerned that His will be done in this matter of having a united Church to confirm with full effectiveness the Gospel which He proclaimed. As long as Christian people are willing to denounce one another and manifest antagonism to one another, they cannot demonstrate what God wishes to do for society as a whole. And that demonstration is most urgently needed. If today in all the world there were one Church binding all who profess to be Christians into one community, in which all would esteem others better than themselves, can we doubt that the world would accept this as a demonstration of what God wants to do for all men, or that there would follow a universal turning away from man-made creeds with their idolatry and human weakness to Christ?

In a South Indian village I asked many men what difference Christ had made in their lives. The answer of one of them has stayed with me. It was, "Christ found us lower than the dogs. He made us men." It thrilled me that he did not use the personal "I." He was talking of a beloved community. Christ had found a pathetic group of people in this man's village, people who had suffered much at the hands of their fellows. They were despised Outcastes, vicious in many of their ways, dirty in their habits, illiterate, and many of them diseased. He called them out of their degradation. He broke the inhibitions that bound them. He lifted the sense of hopelessness from their minds. He healed many of their diseases. He gave them a new picture of themselves as the beloved of God. He exchanged their sense of grievance for a sense of mission. He made them the Church. So this lad said, "We were worse than dogs. He made us men." Their changed lives as individuals, the enriched life of their homes and their changed position in the village in relation to other communities were recognized and unhesitatingly admitted and praised by everyone in the village, except for one crusty old landlord who grumbled that they were upstarts who had fooled everybody except him. He added, "Underneath they can't be very different from what they were. So our religion teaches us. But they certainly act differently and I don't like it. If they were still as they were formerly, they'd work for me for a quarter of what I have to pay now to get my work done."

In a Japanese prison camp in Indonesia an impressive demonstration was made of the power of the Church to confirm the Gospel amid the hatreds and multiplied evils of war. One of the prisoners was a Brahman soldier from North India, captured when Singapore fell. He knew next to nothing of Christianity, but was observant and studious. For the first time he was thrown in prolonged close contact with Christians. He discovered that some of them stood the strain of prison life remarkably well and soon noted that they were the ones whom he often saw reading their Bibles and meeting to sing and pray. He noted, too, that among the prison guards were two who took no part in the brutalities inflicted upon the prisoners by their fellow guards and learned that they were Christians. After a while he talked to two British soldiers and they invited him to join them in reading the Bible and in worship. These observations and experiences led him to become a diligent student of the Bible and soon he felt a sense of community with all whom he recognized as Christians. Before long he was an avowed believer and a witness to Christ and in time he brought several other imprisoned Hindu soldiers to Christ. When released he returned to India and quickly sought an opportunity to unite with the Church. I baptized him in Delhi, but his conversion was due to the Christian witness of the Church across the borders of race and strife. The oneness in the love of Christ of the Japanese prison guards and the British soldiers had overcome the strains of war and imprisonment and political unrest, and brought him to

The Confirmation of the Gospel

Christian faith, purpose and experience.

Those Japanese guards and their British prisoners were not ordained ministers, but as laymen in the Church they accepted the obligation to bear witness to Christ. The command to preach and prove the Gospel was given to the entire Church and is an obligation of all Christians. The evasion of personal responsibility in this matter of confirming the Gospel is a very common practice. "Leave it to the preacher" and "Let the women do the work" are two popular methods of evasion that disastrously retard the progress of the Church and prevent the conversion of multitudes. As an illustration of what one layman, a very underprivileged layman, can do, consider the story of a very recent convert from Islam. He was a teacher in a high school in India. He belonged to a community descended from Rajputs (high-caste Hindu farmers and soldiers) who became Muslims about three hundred years ago. They retained many of their Hindu social customs and were never entirely Islamized. The Hindu renaissance led by the Arya Samajists, a sect of Hindu reformers, who have been much influenced by the monotheism and democracy of Islam and Christianity, led many thousands of them back into the ranks of professed followers of Hinduism. This young man's parents and parents-in-law were among those who re-entered Hinduism on profession of that faith. But they and many others were as disappointed with Hinduism as they had been with Islam. Their son began a study of Christianity. After a few months he wanted to become a Christian, but his wife refused. She said she had two religions and that was enough. Her brother had become a Communist. She, too, was inclined that way. When she became seriously ill her husband took her to a Mission Hospital where faithful medical and nursing care saved her life. The personal work of doctors and nurses and the prayers of her husband confirmed the Gospel to her satisfaction. Then husband, wife and children confessed Christ, were baptized and received into the Church. He began immediately to seek the conversion of others. This was in June 1949. Already at this writing, hundreds of the community to which he formerly belonged are responding to his witness. The change in him and his family, and the work he and his new brethren in Christ are doing for them is confirming the Gospel with such effect that scores are attending services and some appear to be looking forward to baptism and membership in the Church.

Another illustration is provided by a very able and recent Brahman convert. He was shocked by the crimes committed in the name of Hinduism, Sikhism and Islam when passions were inflamed by the partition of India. He noticed that leadership in the fighting within the Hindu, Sikh and Muslim communities came from the more religious persons in each group, and that opposition to the killing came mainly from less religious persons. In disgust he concluded that religion was an evil influence, and made a tentative approach to Communism, but the instruction given to him by Communists made a virtue of violence, and he concluded that Communism, with its planned killing, would be even worse than the religions which allowed and condoned killing in the heat of communal passion. In this state of mind he began an enquiry into Christianity. He had seen Christians saving the lives of Hindus, Sikhs and Muslims during the post-partition disturbances. Indeed his own life had been saved by Christians and he had failed to realize the significance of the fact. He had been inclined to consider that there are good people and bad people everywhere all the time and he was fortunate in that good people had found him and saved his life. Why the Christians were good people, willing to risk their lives to save him, did not become an issue in his mind at once. But when he began to study Christianity, reading the Bible and talking with Christians, he learned lessons to which he had been blind. He has now been blessedly converted. Within the first year of his experience as a Christian he led more than a score of people to Christ. His work for Christ knows no bounds of caste. Brahmans, Untouchables, Sikhs, Muslims, Communists, and nominal Christians share his attention and hear his witness.

The Church in India has produced many heroic pastors. I think of a young man who was born in one of the most degraded and oppressed castes of Untouchables, but attended a Christian Boarding School from which he emerged a high school graduate, intelligent, confident, poised and eager for service. He trained for the ministry. When young men of the caste in which he was born, converted as he had been but not educated as he was, were recruited to work as scavengers in the army, which would not provide them with a chaplain to accompany them and look after their spiritual needs, he enlisted as a scavenger in order that he might go with them and minister unto them. For many who have escaped from the social degradation, ignominy and oppression of India's Scavenger castes death itself would be preferable to return to their status, yet for the sake of Christ and this little section of His Church, and in fulfillment of his sense of vocation, this young man who had slowly climbed the steeps returned to the depths.

Another young minister, burdened for a group of Sweepers, asked that he be appointed to be their pastor and be made wholly dependent upon them for his living. He had come from among the Sweepers, but had established himself in an independent respected position as a minister, and had won to Christ a Brahman woman whom he had subsequently married. Yet he had such a sense of pastoral vocation, and his wife had so fully entered into his ministry, that they went back among the Sweepers to live with them, share all their troubles, and eat and wear what they could provide, and for over twenty years this devoted couple has served them with gratifying results.

That many who call themselves Christians, and are known as such, fail to show in their characters, their personalities, or their way of life the evidences that prove the Gospel, is as true in India as it is in other countries. But the discriminating Indian observer often recognizes that such people, so far from disproving the Gospel, prove only that they do not put it to the test in their lives. When an eminent national leader on one occasion denied that Christians are any better than non-Christians, a prominent Hindu appealed to him to come to his village and see what changes for the better had followed the conversion of the Untouchables of his village. He said, "Many whom you know as Christians may be very unworthy and disappointing people, but I know the Gospel which they profess to believe works, for I have seen its power demonstrated in many people in my village. What I have seen has made me a believer and I hope some time to know personally what they know of Christ's salvation." Those changes, and the redemptive experiences that made them possible, do not just happen. They follow the coming of the Church, and are rightly interpreted as confirmations of the Gospel through the Church.

CHAPTER VII

The Continuing Need for Confirmation

The Confirmation of the Gospel

With the Gospel so amply proved in history it may seem strange to read of a continuing need for its confirmation. But the fact remains that most people now living are either unacquainted with the Gospel or are unconvinced that it is true.

St. Paul realized a continuing need for confirmation even when he was in the midst of his effective apostolic labors. He wrote to the Church at Philippi "For the defense and confirmation of the Gospel ye are partakers with me of grace." So soon after the Resurrection and Pentecost he realized that individuals and congregations would have to provide living confirmations of the Gospel if they were to communicate its truth to others. He was confident that his own life and ministry proved what he preached, and that it was so by the grace of God; and that by the grace given to them his fellow believers could offer the same evidence in their own lives.

A South Indian pastor preached one day about the conversion of Saul of Tarsus and in the course of his sermon told of other notable conversions, among them of St. Augustine and of John Wesley. Later a Hindu, who had heard him, said "Your sermon was eloquent. It seems that your religion has worked well in a few lives in other countries in times past, but what proof can you give that it works in India now?" In California one day I told of some then recent conversions in India, and a layman in tones of distress said "We are told that conversions like that have happened in America too, but I have not known of them in my church or in any other church in my town. Why?" The American, as well as the Indian, needed living confirmations of the Gospel, and their need is common to all men everywhere. Christian experience cannot be maintained at its best without constant renewal, and that continuing consciousness of the Grace of God working within oneself, and evidence that it is at work in others, are both very helpful. The Church that does not see the Gospel confirmed in changed character and enriched personality is not enjoying normal health.

A few years ago a young man completed a course of study for the ministry in a theological seminary in India. To my surprise his district superintendent did not want to give him an appointment in his district. The reason given was that the young man would be handicapped in his work by the bad character of his relatives. Both parents had misbehaved in their youth, an uncle was in jail, and a sister was suspected of immorality. However, the District Superintendent expressed confidence in the character and ability of the young man. Yielding to his judgment I arranged an appointment for the young man in another Annual Conference. There his ministry was wonderfully blessed. When, a few years later, I visited the small town where he then lived and cared for a fairly large congregation, and from where he ministered to a dozen small congregations in out-lying villages, I was welcomed by a representative Committee of Citizens, which included Hindus and Muslims, to thank me for sending him there as a pastor. "This man," said they, "has made us all love Jesus Christ. He is a holy man. He has given us a new idea of what God is like and of what He wants us to be. Keep him here many years and we will all become new men and women." That pastor was confirming the Gospel day after day. Learning all this I wondered what those who had spoken of him with such admiration and affection would think if they knew of his family and former caste background! I did not wonder long for one of the town's leading citizens remarked "This pastor tells us that he comes from among the Untouchables and that some members of his own family are wicked. How can such be? Surely Christ must be all that you missionaries claim that He is when He can make a man like this young preacher out of such material as the Outcastes!"

The Confirmation of the Gospel

Man is a strange compound of reason and emotion. This is especially true in respect to religion. Few men respond to the call of religion because of reason alone. The reasoning processes of Hindus, Muslims, Sikhs, Parsees, Jews and Christians may differ a little, but they are subjected to very different forms of religious emotion. These differences are not basic in their natures, but are developed by different processes of training and by divergent experiences. Religion is not communicated so effectively by logical syllogisms as by social contacts. No amount of confirmation of the Gospel by reason alone, or by facts drawn out of the history of another race in a former generation is likely to bring persons brought up in another religious community to Christian faith unless it is communicated by one who is, himself, in some degree, a living confirmation of that Gospel.

Religion spreads on social lines. One is influenced more strongly by persons with whom he feels a community of interest than by others. It follows, then, that evangelists are needed in every community. The conversion of a school mate, proved by his change of character, will do more to convince a group of students than will an essay on the miracles of Jesus, or on the Resurrection, or on Pentecost. To say this is not to deny the power of the written word, or the appeal of history to the mind and heart, but to affirm the need for local confirmation of the relevancy of the Gospel to the individual, whoever he is and wherever he is. The confirmation of the Gospel in the lives of people known and regarded as their own is the explanation of its acceptance by closely-knit social groups as in the mass movements of India and the tribal movements to Christ in many lands.

This chapter is being written shortly after a visit to Sarawak where a revival of great power is in progress among the people known as Ibans, or Sea-Dyaks. In a tribal long-house, in which there live some twenty families – their living quarters adjoined and one wide verandah running the entire length of the settlement – I enquired why all but three families had confessed Christian faith and joined the Church. The answer came clearly "One man became a Christian. From this experience some of us learned, and joined him as believers. As more people proved in their own lives that the new religion is good, still others came to Christ. Now the three remaining families are convinced, and our friends and relatives in other long-houses know that Christ is Lord and Savior and they, too, are asking for the Gospel." From that long-house we went to another in answer to an urgent invitation. There we found thirteen families united in the purpose to accept Christ. But in a thin third long-house where there were many Christians we met an old man who said "These other people seem to be happy in their new faith. It may be good for them but would it be good for me? I don't know. None of my own family has been converted. I'll wait until one of them becomes a Christian and if he tells me that it is good then I may also try the new way. Until then I'll hold on to the gods and demons I already know."

It is not in compact social groups alone that confirmation in contemporary life is required if men are to be saved. Nor is the effect of the individual's confirmation of the Gospel entirely limited to those within his own group. When the power of Christ to remake men is clearly shown in a disciple's changed character and mode of living, the effect is sometimes shown in the most unexpected places. A landlord and his son, in a South Indian village, quarreled violently and the son left home in anger. Among the landlord's servants was a man of evil repute. One day he came to his master with the surprising information that he had become a Christian, and that he proposed to repay the landlord for various things he had stolen from him. He had no money with which to pay at once but he confessed his sins and promised to begin making regular payments immediately and to continue them till the whole debt was paid. His employer was amazed to hear the confession and the promise to repay. He was more amazed when the servant actually gave him four rupees. Within two years the entire amount stolen had been paid up. Moreover the servant was in every way a better man, more industrious, cleaner and apparently more intelligent. The landlord, seeking an explanation, bought a Bible and a while later began attending the church in the village. He was at length convinced of the truth of the Gospel and, confessing his faith, was baptized by the pastor who had been an Untouchable. He then went in search of his son and, finding him, showed himself so changed that the son also was convinced of the power of Christ. Together then, the father, the son, the servant, and the pastor and the congregation of former Untouchable Hindus confirmed the Gospel so convincingly that scores of local residents, representing nearly all castes, accepted the claims of Christ and gave their hearts to Him.

A young Brahman whose father was principal of a high school, came into close association with many Christians. The son was of an enquiring mind and read the Bible frequently and studiously. It interested him deeply. He talked to his father who urged him to stop reading the book, saying "It is attractive but it is not true. Look at the Christians here – they are no better than we Brahmans. On the contrary, many of them live very unworthy lives. If the so-called Gospel were true these Christians would be much better than they are." "But" said the son "do we not hear constantly that the misconduct of Hindus does not prove the Hinduism is wrong? You want me to judge our Hindu religion only by the character and life of the best Hindus, men like Mahatma Gandhi. Let us see if the claims of Christ are proved by any of His disciples." An intensive study of local Christians made him conclude sadly that very few of them were any better than the average Hindu or Muslim. But he was deeply impressed by one family – the pastor, his wife and their daughters. They seemed to live as the Bible taught. The father of this little family, a converted Hindu from a highly respected upper caste, was a humble, God-fearing man, patriotic, unselfish, kind and gentle in spirit. The mother and two daughters were like him. Their home life was beautiful to behold. The young man's heart was "strangely warmed." Here was evidence for which he was seeking. He confessed his faith and was baptized at the cost of being disowned by his family, but he became radiant in his joy as a Christian. That radiance led a young Sikh graduate teaching in a high school, to renew his interest in Christianity that he had suppressed since his days as a college student, and he too was converted. These two young men, along with the daughter of the pastor – now married to the former Brahman – are among the most active and effective members of the Church in the North India city where they now live.

Underlying the Christian Gospel is a principle of personal responsibility which men generally have been very slow to accept. The Jewish prophets gave some intimations of recognition of this principle but before Christ few in Israel grasped its truth. The disciples experienced persistent difficulty in accepting it. The Church, even in this twentieth century, still evinces some difficulty in accepting its basic implications. There is, for example, a tendency to leave evangelism to men in the ministry. Often the new convert is more easily able to present the evangel to the unconverted than is the old established Christian, and the layman can often more effectively evangelize his associates than can the pastor. Bishop Azariah, one of the most successful evangelists of this century, succeeded in winning the co-operation of the laity in his diocese as few ministers have ever done. He did this by stressing at every opportunity the personal responsibility of every Christian to present Christ to others both by word and life. When he had baptized new converts he would ask them to place their hands on their own heads and say after him "I am a Christian. Woe to me if I do not preach the Gospel to others." And he interpreted preaching as presenting the Gospel by every means in one's power. "Your life must prove what your tongue speaks about the saving power of Jesus Christ." If the whole Church would begin now to confirm the Gospel by testimony of word and life vast numbers who have remained skeptical would be convinced quickly, with results which would make the ingathering that followed the first Pentecost seem small by comparison.

Several characteristics of the present world situation contribute to an expanding opportunity in evangelism. Of these, three are outstanding and interrelated: a) the rise of democracy with its demand for equality of opportunity, b) the weakening of hierarchies and systems of reserved rights and privileges, and c) the peculiar position occupied by the English language as the vehicle of the distinctive culture of the age. In an imposed government opportunity for individual decision on matters of religion may be wholly denied or severely restricted. Where Islam is in power in governments even today, there are strict laws against the right of Muslims to change their religion. But to the extent that democracy has become real and not merely nominal, interference with personal religious freedom is resented. In other lands there is, on the part of governments professing democratic ideals and recognizing the growing strength of democracy, a fear of the consequences to them if religious freedom is restricted. Even the Communist governments of Russia and China seem to be doing some serious rethinking of their attitudes toward religion. Both have apparently abandoned former programs of active all out opposition to religion. In India religious liberty is guaranteed formally by the Constitution, but stronger than the constitutional guarantee is the awakened sense of individuality among the people. Men and women who recently thought of themselves as members of the caste or a tribe, subjects of custom, their destiny determined in advance by their birth into a certain status, are now conscious of their rights and responsibilities as persons. Even in the villages if one now asks a stranger "Who are you?" he is not as sure as of old to get such an answer as "We are Brahmans" or "We are Chamars" but may be told "People call me Pritam Lal" or even "My name is Kishan Singh." This new sense of individuality is, to some extent, a by-product of the franchise. When people of importance whom the villager formerly could only see at a distance now come to him to solicit his vote, the effect on him outlasts the election and extends into many areas outside his political thinking. A man made conscious of his worth as a voter and sought after by the politician is not easily kept subservient to the priest or the landlord or the caste, or even the elders in his family, in respect to religion. Another result of the introduction of democracy in India that helps to open many minds and hearts for the Gospel is the removal of the sense of grievance about foreign rule. As long as Britain ruled, many patriots were not willing to consider Christianity, which they knew to be the religion professed by most Britishers, as having any possible value for them. Resentment effectively blocked the way for the Good News to reach them. Now that they are in the proud position of exercising, along with their fellow citizens, ultimate political authority and are grateful that Britain yielded control peacefully, the old block is gone and the way is open. Indeed many are today very friendly to their former rulers and are inclined to an appreciation of all things British, including their religion.

The decline of hierarchies and systems of reserved power and privilege has occurred all over the world, but nowhere more than in India. Caste, as it developed in India, was the most elaborate and thorough hierarchical system that man ever devised. Brahmans have possessed a rare genius for obtaining authority and handing it on to their children and their children's children. They made the priesthood their monopoly, but did not bar themselves from any position of high privilege and power. Subordinate to themselves, but to no others, they placed the Kshatriyas and below them the Vaishyas or merchants, and below them the Sudras, or artisans – who were superior only to the Mlechchas, or Outcastes. In this they differed only in degree of organizing skill and protective farsightedness displayed from the workers of other ancient cultures. Greece, for example, had their nobles, free-men and slaves, and even the philosophers Aristotle and Plato accepted the institution of slavery as essential to the development of a leisured class, capable of a high level of culture. Slowly, and largely because of Hebrew-Christian influence teaching the worth of the individual and his personal responsibility, the ancient cultures everywhere have changed. Slavery has disappeared except in a few dark corners of the world, and the more refined systems of reserving power and privilege, and of imposing disabilities and deprivations, are in process of disintegration. The breakdown of caste in India is progressively freeing multitudes from long-established inhibitions. This applies to the beneficiary castes as much as to the victim castes. Brahmans are being freed along with Harijans. Indeed, more Brahmans than Harijans are exercising their new freedom in investigating religion. It is safe to say that currently more Brahmans are being converted to Christ every year than in any ten years before India achieved Independence.

English has become pre-eminently the vehicle of the culture of this age. What Sanskrit was, from the borders of Persia to the farthest reaches of the East Indies in the period of Hinduism's greatest power, and Arabic was for several centuries in the Dark Ages of Medievalism, and French was in diplomacy in the eighteenth and first half of the nineteenth centuries – all that and much more has English become in our times. All over the world there is an insatiable hunger for understanding and use of this language. In India the desire to know English has grown immensely since Independence. During the struggle for Independence many patriots resolved to restrict the teaching of English. The language seemed to them the badge of their subservience to an alien government. Few of them went so far as to keep their own children from learning it, yet they had no hesitation in proposing to prevent other peoples' children from learning the language. Now Hindi is proclaimed as the official language of the government of India, and of a number of state governments. But the demand for English has spread to every part of the Republic. When there is no pressure from the government upon anyone to learn this language of the former rulers the people are demanding that facilities be provided for their children to learn it. This position in India is more or less duplicated in many other countries. It is reported that even in China the demand of English has grown significantly during this past decade.

In much of Asia and Africa English is the chief linguistic vehicle of evangelism. This is due, in a small part, to the fact that English is the mother tongue of a majority of foreign missionaries working in these countries. But it is due even more to the abundance and excellence of Christian literature available in English. The Bible Society of India sells more copies of the Bible printed in English than in Hindi. Enquirers coming to missionaries in search of information about Christ or the Church, if they have a choice of languages to be used in the conversation, almost invariably choose English. This is neither by way of subtle pleasing of the missionary, nor because of a desire to display proficiency in the use of English so much as it is due to a feeling that Christianity is more authentically expressed in English than in those languages of India into which it has been introduced in the modern missionary era, and where translations are, as yet, far from satisfactory. The words which translators are forced to use as the best available for their purpose are often very imperfect instruments, being mere approximations to the concepts they are used to convey. In the course of time in lands where Christianity has been widely accepted the words used adjust themselves to Christian meanings, but in the presence of living non-Christian religions for the purpose of which they were originally formed, they may continue to convey Christian concepts very imperfectly.

The need for confirming the Christian Gospel afresh for the vastly enlarged number in all parts of the world who are now using the English language, is intensified by the uses to which the secular press is putting the language. Newsgathering agencies keep the world informed of sensational developments everywhere. Crime news can be made sensational, generally, and very often the report of some crime causes a greater stir half way around the world than in an adjoining state. The new democracies are especially susceptible to shock by accounts of racial strife or political corruption in the older democracies, and the enemies of democracy are shrewd enough to broadcast widely lurid and often quite exaggerated descriptions of such occurrences. The high divorce rate in the USA is discussed in all parts of the world about as much as in America. A typical response came to my attention as this chapter was being written. A young Parsee, en route to an American University for post-graduate study, lamented the breakdown of family life in the States, estimating the proportion of marriages that end in divorce as fifty percent. He expressed much surprise and relief in having come to know several American couples who appeared to be happily married!

On the other hand, much that is helpful is being done through the use of English by secular agencies. Christian organizations and individuals make available to the press of many nations material that counteracts evil impulses and encourages the virtues of faith, hope, and charity. Even the much and justly criticized Hollywood moving picture industry has sent over the world some very helpful pictures. <u>The King of Kings</u> has drawn appreciative audiences in all parts of the world, ever since it was produced a generation ago. After seeing it a Hindu High Court Judge asked the writer how much the missionary societies had paid to have it produced. He thought it was doing more to turn people to Christ than could a hundred good missionaries. <u>Ben Hur</u> and <u>The Robe</u> have also undergirded the Christian witness. Through schools and private reading there has come extensive acquaintance with noble Christian characters, ministerial and lay, and with Christian literature. St. Francis of Assissi and Francis Xavier, of the Roman Church, and Martin Luther and John Wesley, among Protestants, have been taken into the hearts of many non-Christians. Christ is often so loved and revered that many Hindus and Buddhists object to being called non-Christians. In the political sphere George Washington, Thomas Jefferson, and Abraham Lincoln are beloved heroes of the democratic faith as truly in Delhi, Tokyo, Jakarta, Johannesburg, Seoul and Manila as in Washington.

When Dr. Billy Graham preached in India early in 1956 his audiences were reported by the newspapers as ranging from six thousand to one hundred twenty thousand in different cities. Multitudes had read in the daily papers about his meetings in America and

Europe and wanted to hear the man who was understood to be responsible for the conversion of so many to Christ. Among those who responded to his invitation to accept Christ were thousands who had never before made public confession of Christian faith. Among them were Hindus, Muslims, Sikhs, lawyers, business men, teachers and government officials. Although Dr. Graham's sermons were translated into local languages approximately half of all who heard him understood his own English delivery. It was much the same in other Asian countries. Except where the interpreters were exceedingly good the net gain through their use was slight.

In the world situation of today, the opportunities available for effective presentation of the Good News of the Kingdom to the nations are greater than in any previous generation the Church has known. However, their maximum use is not possible unless a great many Christians will undertake non-professional missionary service, supporting themselves by whatever honest work they can do best, but dedicating their effort to the proclamation and confirmation of the Gospel. And even more is maximum success dependent upon the enrichment of Christian experience through the Church. The nineteenth century is rightly called the Great Century in Christian Missions. But the second half of the twentieth century will be incomparably greater if the above conditions are met, for multitudes in every country await proof that Christ is able to meet their need for a Lord and Savior.

The Confirmation of the Gospel

The Confirmation of the Gospel

ACKNOWLEDGEMENTS

Many hands are needed to bring forth a manuscript from text to final publication, even a small one.

Morgan Tracy first found and brought the manuscript to my attention. His enthusiasm for the Archives – and *The Foundry* – was the motivating force behind getting this hidden work out into the light of day. He also faithfully provided editorial assistance all along the way.

Suzanne Gehring for her tireless processing and organizing of our historical material, and Asbury University alumnus *Caleb Conover* for his help in analyzing the Pickett Collection.

Asbury University student worker *Hossana Miranda*, who transferred the typed printed manuscript into digital formatting and helped with the initial editing.

BJ Haas and *Doug Butler* for further refining and editing the manuscript into its current form.

Brad Easley, formerly with the University Marketing and Communication Office, for his creativity and work on the design and layout.

A special note of thanks to the *Mr. and Mrs. William R. Gardner (Elizabeth Guess) Endowed Professorship for the Promotion of Holiness* at Asbury University, which provided the necessary funding for the publication of this work in book form.